John Campbell Colquhoun

The Progress of the Church of Rome towards ascendency in England

Traced through the parliamentary history of nearly forty years

John Campbell Colquhoun

The Progress of the Church of Rome towards ascendency in England
Traced through the parliamentary history of nearly forty years

ISBN/EAN: 9783744745611

Printed in Europe, USA, Canada, Australia, Japan

Cover: Foto ©Lupo / pixelio.de

More available books at **www.hansebooks.com**

THE PROGRESS OF THE CHURCH OF ROME

TOWARDS

ASCENDENCY IN ENGLAND,

TRACED

THROUGH THE PARLIAMENTARY HISTORY OF NEARLY FORTY YEARS.

BY

JOHN CAMPBELL COLQUHOUN.

(PUBLISHED FOR THE NATIONAL PROTESTANT UNION.)

LONDON:
WILLIAM MACINTOSH, 24, PATERNOSTER-ROW;
AND OF ALL BOOKSELLERS.
1868.
PRICE ONE SHILLING.

"Lo, Rome herself, proud mistress now no more
Of arts, but thundering against heathen lore;
Her greyhair'd Synods cursing books unread,
And Bacon trembling for his brazen head.
And see, my son, the hour is on its way
That lifts our goddess to imperial sway;
This favourite isle, long severed from her reign,
Dove-like she gathers to her wings again.
Behold yon isle, by Palmers, pilgrims trod,
Men bearded, bald, cowl'd, uncowl'd, shod, unshod,
Peel'd, patch'd, and pyebald, linsey-wolsey brothers,
Grave mummers, sleeveless some, and shirtless others.
Around her chiefs a sable army stand,
A low-born, cell-bred, selfish, servile band,
Prompt or to guard or stab, to saint or damn,
Heaven's Swiss, who fight for any god or man.
Through Lud's fam'd gates, along the well-known Fleet,
Rolls the black troop, and overshades the street;
Till showers of sermons, characters, essays,
In circling fleeces whiten all the ways.
And still cries Rome, if more devotion warms,
'Down with the Bible, up with the Pope's arms!'"

—Pope's Dunciad.

PREFACE.

When a question falls into the hands of political parties it is apt to become distorted. Men refuse to see facts which are palpable, and, in the heat of passion, they deny what, in a calmer mood, they would admit to be undeniable. We have an example of this state of the public mind at the present moment. One party affirms that Rome is making great strides to power; another party derides this as an idle tale. The principles of our Protestant Constitution, nay of the Reformation, tremble in the balance, say some. Don't raise that silly cry, say others; kick out of the way the dead horse of Popery, says Mr. Spurgeon. It seems to me, says our shrewd Premier, that the real cry is no Protestantism.

In such a temper of the public mind the wisest expedient is to turn from political excitement to historical narrative; from party violence to the calmness of a dispassionate review. I will engage that my statement of facts shall be accurate, and all I ask from my reader is a fair hearing. I address all parties without distinction, Liberals as well as Conservatives, the honest Nonconformist as well as the Churchman.

Chartwell,
    September 1, 1868.

CHAPTER I.

OUR DANGER.

Two things I premise. When statesmen laugh at the notion that Protestantism is in danger, I lay before them the following evidence :—The late Sir Robert Peel certainly was not a fanatic. He was eminently a cool and sagacious politician. None can say that he was an ultra-Protestant. Yet, in the year 1838 he made this remark, in my hearing, to a deputation from Scotland, that he thought the time was coming, nay was near, when we would have to fight over again the battle of the Reformation, and he drew this conclusion from the movement of Archbishop Droste in Prussia, and from the difficulties which the claims of Rome were occasioning to the Prussian, the Austrian, and the Baden Governments. How much more serious would have been his apprehension had he lived till our day, and seen what we see!

The late Robert P and Dr. ning.

For two events are passing before us, which would have struck him as they have struck Dr. Manning. Dr. Manning tells us, that there is within the Church of England a section who save him and his priests the trouble of polemical controversy, a section who abjure the name and doctrines of Protestantism, and adopt the rites and dogmas of Rome :—

"In the last thirty years," says Dr. Manning, "there has sprung up in the Anglican Establishment an extensive rejection of Protestantism, and a sincere desire and claim to be Catholic..... Protestantism is recognized as a thing intrinsically untenable and irreconcilable with the Catholic faith. The school of which I speak claim to be Catholic, because they reject Protestantism with all its heterodoxies...... At this time the doctrine of the Sacraments, their nature, number, and grace; the intercession and invocation of saints; the power of the priesthood in sacrifice and absolution; the excellence and obligations of the religious life, are all held and taught by clergymen of the Church of England..... Add to this the practice of confession, and of works of temporal and spiritual mercy, in form and by rule borrowed from the Catholic Church, all are to be found among those who are still within the Anglican communion. I must also add the latest and strangest phenomenon of this movement—the adoption of an elaborate ritual with its vestments borrowed from the Catholic Church." *

Dr. Manning further speaks of the effect on the congregations produced by the teaching and practices of these clergymen, and he speaks of it in the following words:—

"The multitude worshipping in churches which might almost be mistaken for ours . . . is very great. They are coming up to the very threshold of the Church. They have learned to lean upon it as the centre of Christendom, from which they sprang, and upon which their own Church is supposed to rest. They use our devotions, our books, our pictures of piety. They are taught to believe the whole Council of Trent, not indeed in its own true meaning, but in a meaning invented by their teachers." †

Such is Dr. Manning's description of the Romish party within our Church; and the effect of Rome on the literature, politics, and society of England is not less remarkable. Dr. Manning corroborates the testimony of the late Cardinal Wiseman at the Congress of Malines. He says that Romish principles are spreading into our books, our engravings, and our newspapers:—

"Thousands, who would not for the world set foot in a Romish Church, read photographic descriptions of high masses, and requiems, and consecrations, processions, pilgrimages, and canonizations. The air is full of it. Call it a plague of flies, of frogs, or of boils. It is upon man and beast; throw ashes into the air, it comes down Popery." ‡

These testimonies, one from a great statesman, the other from the chief member of the Church of Rome in England, are impressive. There is evidently no exaggeration, and when I hear an eloquent Dissenter deride the dead horse of Popery, I am inclined to inquire whether the nag ridden by Mr. Miall and his allies, which Mr. Spurgeon says is half-starved in the Dissenting stable, or the well-fed steed from the Vatican stalls, is most likely to win the Derby in our national race?

Liberation Society on endowments. There is another hint I offer. The Liberationists think they will get rid of endowments by their alliance with the Church of Rome; they will forgive me if I express my fear that this is a sign of their inexperience and simplicity. They sent a Mission to Ireland

* "Essays on Religion." 2nd Series. Edited by Dr. Manning, pp. 12, 13.

† Ibid., p. 14.   ‡ Ibid., p. 10.

in September, 1867, and, assisted by Mr. O'Neill Daunt, they obtained an assurance from the heads of the Romish Church that they do not want and will not accept endowment for the priests. Is this a satisfactory assurance? Committees of Parliament in 1824 and 1825 were assured by the Romish Bishops that, under no circumstances, would they ever disturb the Irish Church, or the settlement of Irish property; nay, all the Roman Catholic members swore to this, at the table of the House of Commons. Are the whispered promises, made to Mr. Miall and his friends, more reliable than the public pledges given on oath by Romish Bishops and their representatives in the British Parliament? Yet all these have been broken.

I notice another point. There is a very suspicious reserve in the pledges of the Romish Bishops. They disclaim all wish for endowment for their priests, but they have a strong hankering after our money. I observe that in the State of New York they have, by skilful management, extracted enormous sums for their schools, colleges, hospitals, and other institutions, by offering their support to political parties. Are they likely to do less in England? They have already pocketed thousands of the public money for army chaplains and prison chaplains, for Reformatories, for training schools, and national schools under the control of priests, and nuns, and friars. They pressed the Whig Government to give them bursaries and salaries for a College absolutely under the Bishops' control, and, as the Papers now on the table of the House show, they pressed the same demand on Lord Mayo. This looks very like a hankering after public money. If it be said this is not an endowment, by what name shall we call it? If not a Regium it is a Parliamentary Donum. *Romish pretensions.*

Another point strikes me, which I present to the judgment of the intelligent and vigilant among Nonconformists. *Messrs. Gladstone and Bright prepa to endow the Church of Rome.*

If Mr. Gladstone and Mr. Bright succeed, and the Irish Church falls, some millions will be at the disposal of Parliament. Is any part of these to go to Cardinal Cullen and his priests? This question was asked by Mr. Gladstone's Liberal supporters, but it was not answered by him. He replied, but his replies were, like the answers of the Delphic oracle, ambiguous and unintelligible. He was then pressed by a motion, and tested by a vote. Then followed a scene every way remarkable. It was brought on by Mr. Sinclair Aytoun, a Liberal of uncompromising honesty. This quality is not often found in Parliamentary partisans, and it is greatly disliked by Whig leaders. Docility and credulity are the qualities most approved. But Mr. Aytoun's suspicions of the views of Messrs. Bright and Gladstone had been aroused, and they were not to be allayed by general statements. Rumours of secret understandings with Cardinal Cullen were rife, interviews with Dr. Manning were spoken of. The air was full of them. Mr. Gladstone had talked of the Maynooth Grant being removed from the Consolidated Fund. Was this payment to be replaced by four millions of hard cash handed over absolutely to Cardinal Cullen?

There were circumstances calculated to excite suspicion. Slashing into Church funds with bold hands, Mr. Gladstone and Mr. Bright would not touch the endowments of the Church of Rome with their little finger. When in May last Mr. Aytoun moved that no part of the Church funds should go to the Roman Catholic Church, or to Roman Catholic schools, Mr. Bright rose and denounced this in a transport of indignation. He had, during the recess, said that a lump of money given to a church was no endowment, and now he rebuked all attack on the Roman Catholic Church. The Romish members joined eagerly the shout against Mr. Aytoun. Mr. Gladstone bitterly condemned the Motion. Seeing, however, the temper of the House, he had to put up Mr. Whitbread to move that, with the disestablishment of the Irish Church, the grants to Maynooth and to the Presbyterians must cease. But this was no security; the lump of four millions might still be given to Cardinal Cullen; on this point the words of Dr. M'Cosh were remembered. Dr. M'Cosh was a keen voluntary; he had no sympathy with the Irish Church. He had had much connection with the leaders of Mr. Gladstone's party, and he had written and printed this remarkable warning:—

"I have made it a matter of duty, in these important times, to put myself in communication with some of those who have been leading and guiding the movement for Disendowment. They, one and all, assured me that the principle of equality of all sects being now adopted in Ireland, they must, *if any sum be given to one sect, give a like sum to all in proportion to their population.* Thus, if there be six millions left, after paying personal rights to the Established Church, the Presbyterian Church, and the Catholics for Maynooth, *then four and a half millions must go to the Catholics,* leaving one and a half millions for the various Protestant bodies."*

---

* "The Duty of Irish Presbyterians." By J. M'Cosh, LL.D., Belfast, 1868. See also the "Freeman's Journal," 11th June, 1868, where Sir John Gray

Read in this light, with this commentary, the words of Mr. Bright and the mysterious utterances of Mr. Gladstone become plain. Life-interests are to be dealt with on both sides, but Maynooth professors and students will receive a far larger consideration than the plundered rectors and starving curates; but, after life-interests have been cared for, Mr. Gladstone will propose to Parliament to hand over *four millions and a half* to Cardinal Cullen, to educate (we shall see hereafter what that means) the Irish people after the pleasure of the Romish Church.

No wonder that Mr. Aytoun was not satisfied with Mr. Whitbread's Motion. This Motion was followed by one of Mr. Greene, who proposed to add to Mr. Whitbread's proviso, that no part of the funds of the Irish Church should be appropriated to endow the institutions of any other religious communion; against this Mr Bright spoke with rancorous indignation, and both he and Mr. Gladstone struggled fiercely, *and voted against it.*

On the 5th of June another ray of light was let into the cloud which closely covers Mr. Gladstone's future policy. On going into Committee on the Suspensory Bill, Mr. Sinclair Aytoun moved an instruction. It was reasonable; it was in strict analogy with the treatment of the Irish Church; Maynooth with its trustees was to be dealt with on the same terms. But this would not do; a very different fate awaits Cardinal Cullen. So Cardinal Cullen's friends hastened to resist the proposal. Colonel Greville Nugent, a representative of the Priests, was put up to oppose it. Mr. Bright was silent: the boisterous orator is a little too frank when a reserved policy is required. But Mr. Gladstone hurried to the rescue, for he may be trusted to involve in a cloud of words any scheme however indefensible. He was ready with a variety of reasons. The instruction was too large; it was too small; it was singular; it was inequitable; he appealed to the Government, he perplexed the House. He succeeded in bewildering it, and he carried 189 votes against 109. But Colonel Nugent, pressed by the arguments in the debate, had offered that every official in Maynooth should hold his office subject to the pleasure of Parliament. This was evidently fair, but Mr. Gladstone treats Rome with special favour; he found many reasons

lets out what the Roman Catholic Church looks for. The "Daily Review," a Scotch Liberal paper, stated *that Mr. Gladstone was negotiating with Dr. Cullen, and had agreed to give a large sum to the Romish Church,* and this was never contradicted.

against this proposal. Colonel Nugent, therefore, under Mr. Gladstone's directions, was prepared to drop his offer, but this the House would not suffer. Mr. Hardy said the Motion was only reasonable, and with great reluctance Messrs. Gladstone and Bright saw Maynooth placed somewhat on the same footing as the Irish Church. The instruction, at Mr. Gladstone's suggestion, was extended to the Presbyterians, for any fate is good enough for Protestants; it is Rome only which the leaders cover with their shield.

Whatever care Mr. Gladstone has taken to conceal his future intentions with regard to Ireland, his real design of establishing the Church of Rome in Ireland, and enriching it with the spoils of the Protestant Church, appears from his own speeches in the provinces. All that is necessary is to translate his vague and misty language into plain English.

In the speech which he delivered in Southport (*Times*, December 20, 1867,) after complaining that the National endowments of Ireland are given exclusively to the religion of a small number of persons, while the multitude of the poor are left to shift for themselves, he goes on thus :—

"Now I must express to you my firm conviction that *principles of religion must be established in Ireland*, and that it is vain to look to a true union and harmony between that country and this until the Legislature of this country shall have made up its mind to govern and *attain that great consummation*. It may involve the sacrifice of our pride, there may be difficulties to encounter on the way, and there are those who would tell us that it is hostile to religion.

"As to the modes of giving effect to this principle I don't enter upon them. I am of opinion they should be dictated, as a general rule, by that which may appear to be the mature, well-considered, and *general sense of the Irish people.*"

Now this language, if it has any meaning, and it is clear it has, can have only one meaning. Mr. Gladstone had before remarked that Ireland should be treated like Scotland; that is to say, Scotland has a Presbyterian Church endowed; Ireland must have a Romish Church endowed. "For the principles of religion must be established in Ireland," and the "mature and well-considered sense of the Irish people" must be taken and followed. But four millions are subject to the priests, therefore the views of Dr. Cullen and the Bishops must be adopted. No doubt this will involve a "sacrifice of our pride," and some will say it will be "hostile to religion." But it must be done, "that s my conviction," and there is "no other complete and effectual settlement of this great and pressing question."

So much for the future Church to be established in Ireland—but Mr. Gladstone also settles its future education; he says:—

"Ireland has not received up to this hour equal treatment in that matter, and I will tell you how. In this country you are aware the great bulk of parents are in the habit of sending their children to be trained in schools and colleges where the inculcation of the religion to which they belong forms an essential and fundamental part of the instruction that is given."

Then Mr. Gladstone proceeds to show that that has not been done in Ireland, where we have established Secular colleges and National schools. And he goes on:— Mr. Gladstone's secret revealed.

"Now we would not bear that ourselves. I own that if I were prohibited from sending my son to be trained in a school where his religion was taught I should think it a great grievance."

Here then is Mr. Gladstone's remedy for the evils of Ireland. Set up and endow there the Romish Church. Destroy Sir Robert Peel's secular colleges and the National schools. Undo (here we trace the hand of Mr. Bright) all the good that has been done for thirty-eight years; throw back four millions, just emerging from ignorance, into the wretched schools and degrading superstition of the Romish priests; and, inasmuch as large portions of the Irish population have carried with them to America (Mr. Gladstone tells us) "a fierce resentment and inextinguishable aversion to the authority of the Government and the institutions of this country," let that hostile sentiment be instilled into the rising generation throughout Ireland by Romish priests in Romish schools, and then reap what you have sown. His policy Ireland.

If any man, after this speech, feels surprised when Mr. Gladstone shall rise in Parliament hereafter to propose to establish the Church of Rome, endow her with millions of our money, and hand over four millions of Irish to a worse teaching and a more degrading slavery than can be found in Europe outside the Roman States, he has himself to thank for his delusion. And if England adopts Mr. Gladstone's policy for Ireland, she will deserve her doom.

CHAPTER II.

THE PLANS OF THE ROMISH HIERARCHY.

Roman Catholic laity to be distinguished from the hierarchy.

HERE I interpose a caution. When I speak of the Roman party, I by no means confound the Roman Catholic laity with the Roman Priests and Bishops. The views of these two sections are generally identified, but they are distinct; and it would be well if English statesmen would recognise the distinction: one great man, Lord Ormond, did, and, alone of all our statesmen, he governed Ireland and kept it in peace. He separated the Roman Catholic laity from the party of the Priests. The evil is that now the bulk of the Irish Roman Catholic members are returned by the Priests, and therefore they represent in Parliament the ambition and aims of the Priesthood. They are the exponents of the Priests' views, and of the claims of the hierarchy; yet there are thousands of Roman Catholics who groan under the Priests' tyranny and long for deliverance.* They dare not speak, yet occasional pamphlets, and still more private letters, betray their wishes. For these men are loyal, peaceable, and orderly. All that they want is what we want—good government, the supremacy of law, safety for their persons, security for their property, freedom for their minds: these things a good and firm Government ought to give.

But the hierarchy want to rule—they wish to displace our Sovereign, to separate Ireland from England, to hold the reins of power, and then to crush opinion, extinguish conscience, and trample down every spark of free thought under the restraint of an intolerant despotism.

This has been so well stated by an able Liberal in the "Economist" newspaper, on his return from his travels in Ireland (Sept. 24, 1864), that I insert his remarks. After speaking of the progress of improvement in Ireland:—

---

* See Mr. Lowry Whittle's pamphlet on "Free Education." Hodges and Smith, Dublin.

"But Ireland," he says, "still wants one thing, *capital;* it wants the peace which attracts capital; and the good sense, and paramount protecting law, which permits its free application. This is now, perhaps, the crying and central evil of Ireland. Everybody perceives this."

He proceeds:—

"No dispassionate observer, we apprehend, whatever be his political or theological predilections, can shut his eyes to the fact that *the Catholic priesthood,* as at present organized, as at present circumstanced, as at present minded, practically, and to a very sad extent, thwart and impede the progress of the country to a more prosperous condition. Catholic Emancipation was a wise and righteous act. It was an act of justice, an act of policy, an act of necessity. We contended for it at the time, and we have never repented of it since. But no one can maintain that it has borne the beneficent fruits which its advocates prophesied for it. As it is, it cannot be said to have the faintest effect on them in pacifying religious animosities, *in satisfying the desires of the Catholic* hierarchy, in improving their character, enlightening their patriotism, or amending, elevating their influence over the people. *The reverse rather is the case.* They spring, even more exclusively than formerly, from the lowest classes, live more exclusively among them, share more thoroughly and foster more habitually than before all their worst passions and all their narrowest views. There are fewer well-educated and well-mannered men among men. The priests, who are trained at Maynooth, are far inferior in culture to those of former days, and are no better subjects of the British Crown. They take their orders direct from Rome, and consider only the interests of their Church. They vehemently oppose the national system of education from a dread of its *indirectly* proselytising effects, and yet can substitute no other or better in its place. They set their faces against emigration, not unnaturally, because it diminishes their flocks, reduces their stipends, and brings the people under influences adverse to their own. They certainly do nothing to correct, and it is to be feared they do much to encourage the chronic mistrust and the fatal antagonism between the peasant and the landlord; and they do this whether the landlord be Protestant or Catholic. In a word, sad as the admission is, coming from the pen of consistent and sincere Liberals as we have always been, *the priests must now be regarded as the worst enemies the Irish people suffer under.*"

Roman Priests.

This is a remarkable testimony, but I will add to it the evidence of the Romish Prelates themselves.

We remember the Encyclical of the present Pope in 1864. His doctrines appeared to us monstrous in the nineteenth century. But they were natural and consistent. Rome has always held them, and the canons of Rome are unalterable. Their demand is this:—

No religion in a realm but that of Rome. (That was the quarrel of the Roman hierarchy with the late Emperor Maximilian.) No toleration of any faith, or permission to any man to speak, or write, or preach, against the Roman faith.* Absolute deference to the Pope's decrees; obedience to the Papal laws; trials before the Bishops' courts. Are these my words? No! they are Dr. Manning's. He shall speak for himself:—

"If England is ever to be reunited to Christendom it is *by submission to the living authority of the Vicar of Jesus Christ.* The first step of its return must be obedience to his voice, as rebellion against his authority was the first step of its departure." And Dr. Manning says that this time is near. "The Supremacy of our Crown has literally come to nought. The Royal Supremacy has perished by the law of mortality, which consumes all earthly things, and at this period of our history the supremacy of the Vicar of Jesus Christ re-enters, as full of life, as when Henry VIII. resisted Clement VII., and Elizabeth withstood S. Pius V." (Essays on Religion, p. 19.)

With such a prospect before us it is natural to ask how we, poor Protestants, shall stand. Mr. Spurgeon lately published a complaint that Baptist ministers are starving, worse paid than common mechanics. If Rome prevails, his complaint will cease, because Baptist ministers will not be † suffered to minister at all.

Hear on this point Dr. Manning's authority:—

"Hence this principle follows, that neither the Church nor the State, whensoever they are united on the true basis of Divine right, have any cognizance of tolerance. * * * The Church has the right, in virtue of her divine commission, to require of everyone to accept her doctrine. *Whosoever obstinately refuses or obstinately insists upon the election out of it of what is pleasing to himself* is against her. But were the Church to tolerate such an opponent, she must tolerate another. If she tolerate one sect she must tolerate every sect, and thereby give herself up." (Essays, p. 403.)

---

* At this very moment Lord Stanley admits that Julian de Vargas, a Spanish schoolmaster at Malaga, had been confined in a felon's prison, like Matamoras and his friends, for having in his house a Spanish Bible and some French Protestant books. And the Spanish Government had last spring sent a mandate to the Governor of the province of Malaga, directing him to search for Protestant books, to seize their circulators, and deliver them to the tribunals to be punished. (July 21, 1861, Parliamentary Debates.)

† If it is said English laws will always secure toleration, I ask the reader to turn to the facts now occurring in Manchester, and the suppression of mission work in Ireland by violence. (See the case of Mr. Campbell at Athlone.)

THE ROMISH HIERARCHY.

This will show Archdeacon Denison and Dr. Pusey that their coquetting with Rome, mimicking her rites and her dogmas, won't do. Either fall down before the Pope or begone.

If Mr. Spurgeon imagines that his sect may appeal from these dicta to the Courts of Law,* Dr. Manning informs him that an appeal to a civil court is a breach of the Papal law. (Essays, p. 410.) " The civil power is subject to the ecclesiastical." "All princes, as well as people, are subject to the laws and to the canons of the Church, and are to be judged alike by the Supreme Pontiff." To appeal from the judgment of the Pope to an inferior tribunal is " constructive heresy." (Essays, pp. 412, 452.) And if it is said that this is a *brutum fulmen*, Dr. Manning replies, Wait till we get power. " The duty of the civil power is to enforce the laws of the Church, to restrain evil-doers and punish heresy." (Essays, p. 457.)

<small>Mr. Spurgeon.</small>

If Mr. Spurgeon imagines that, driven from his Tabernacle, he may teach in his College, this is a mistake. Cardinal Cullen has shown us in his negotiations with Sir George Grey and with Lord Mayo, that though the State may give money to endow schools, they must not † meddle with them. And here, by Dr. Manning, this principle is laid down and explained.

"The State endows a school, but it must not prescribe the course of education." For "It is astonishing *how small*, in a Christian community, after performing its office of preserving life and property, *is the space rightfully left to the exclusive domination of the civil power.*" (Essays, p. 457.) . . . . " It not only builds hospitals and almshouses, it founds schools, builds churches and monasteries, and endows Episcopal sees." . . . . But here it must stop, for "in so doing, it is acting in a subordinate capacity and with a delegated authority as the helper only, the servant of the spiritual power." (Essays, p. 458.) . . . . Even in passing laws Parliament must defer to the Church. "The State enacts a law, but it must see that it in no way contravenes the higher laws of the Church." ‡

The practical application is plain: the moment that Mr. Spurgeon steps forward to teach in a school, Dr. Manning lays his hand on him. No parent can be suffered to send a son to his college. "The Christian parent is bound to educate the child according to the direction of the Church of Rome." (Essays, p. 458.)

<small>Application of Dr. Manning's Dicta.</small>

---

* The essay is written by Mr. Purcell, but Dr. Manning gives it to the world, as editor, and thus endorses all its statements.

† Dr. McHale has expressed the same view in the plainest language last month (August), and has applied it to the National Schools of Ireland.

‡ All the standard works of Rome say the same. The "Dogmatic Theology," which is used as a class-book for students at Maynooth, teaches the same law. "Tolerantia religiosa est impia et absurda."—Perrone, tom. iii., p. 345. Ed. Louvain, 1838.

Already, even before this power is fully developed, it begins to put forth its feelers. Two Irish members were set up this session to accustom the mind of the House of Commons to these principles of Rome. England has long been inured to a most disorderly freedom; no one has attempted to restrain liberty of discussion; inquiry, and controversy, its natural result, have gone on unchecked.* But these vicious habits must be restrained.

So Mr. Rearden was commissioned to feel the pulses of the House of Commons in this direction. He had not then damaged himself by his indiscreet disloyalty. His day is now over. Rome will find a more wary instrument. On the 16th of May last he put the following question:—

<small>Rome stops Protestant Lectures.</small>

"Mr. Rearden asked the Secretary of State for the Home Department whether it was his intention to introduce a Bill this session for the purpose of preventing lectures *upon the religious profession of faith of any of Her Majesty's subjects in any part of the United Kingdom,* except in churches and chapels licensed for that purpose, and during Divine Service in such churches and chapels, *without first submitting a copy of such lecture* for the approval, revision, and consent of the Secretary of State for the Home Department.

"Mr. HARDY.—I have no intention of introducing such a Bill; and I must protest against adding to the duties of Secretary of State for the Home Department the approval or revision of lectures upon religious subjects. (Hear, hear.)"

But the objects of the Romish hierarchy were not thus to be frustrated. It is well to *educate* the House, to prepare it for what is coming, and to make it consider *restraint of controversy* indispensable. Hereafter, if Messrs. Gladstone and Bright are in power, the final blow will be dealt through the deference of a docile Government. So, on the 21st May, Mr. Maguire, the trusted representative of Cardinal Cullen, the friend and corre-

---

* It is instructive to see that the same system of repression is at work in Prussia. The *Markisches Kirchenblatt* is the organ of the Roman Catholics in Berlin. They publish the most monstrous dogmas on the Divinity of the Virgin. But when a piece was written and prepared to be acted, which exposed the frauds and greed of the Jesuits, the Roman Catholic Bishop interfered at Sigmaringen, and induced the Government to prohibit it; and this Romish newspaper warns the manager of the theatre at Berlin of this, and says that the authorities in Prussia had resolved "not to permit the feelings of nine millions of Catholics to be offended"!! Ever since the war with Austria, this argument has been plied and has prevailed.—*Letter of the Rev. D. Edward from Breslau, June* 9, 1868.

spondent of Mr. Gladstone, addressed to the Home Secretary the following question :—

"NOTICES OF MOTIONS FOR THURSDAY, 21ST MAY, 1868.

"Mr. MAGUIRE.—To ask the Secretary of State for the Home Department whether his attention has been seriously called to the frequent instances of riot and disturbance, injury to person and destruction of property, caused in certain districts of this country by the addresses of a person named Murphy and his colleagues; and whether he can give any assurance to the House that the delivery of such addresses can be prevented for the future." Rome stops liberty of discussion.

Skilful use was made on this occasion of the words and deeds of Mr. Murphy. I say nothing of their character. I neither impugn nor defend them. I receive, with great scepticism, the charges against Mr. Murphy. Till the facts are before us it is impossible to judge; and I am so accustomed to the bold fictions of the Roman priests, that I wait for better evidence than their assertions. But assume that Mr. Murphy was as indiscreet as they assert: so much the better for the priests. Abuse always recoils. It does no harm except to him who uses it. The priests in that case ought to thank the lecturer. But the system of violence, which has been applied to Mr. Murphy, *has been applied uniformly* by Irish priests, under the direction of their bishops, *to harmless persons for many years without any provocation.*

Mr. Maguire complains of Mr. Murphy's words. What does he say to the brutal deeds committed on Irish Romanists, whose only crime is that they wish to read the Bible, and to listen to Protestant preaching? Let him read the facts stated* by Mr. Hobart Seymour; and answer these if he can. If he can't, let him tell me of any country, except Turkey, where such abuses would be endured. When he speaks of violence, let him explain the violence done to Rome crushes conscience.

---

* See a letter to the Earl of Derby by Mr. Hobart Seymour, M.A. (Seeley and Co., 1868.) Mr. Seymour gives the case of three parishes in three parts of Roman Catholic Ireland. In one he cites the efforts of a Roman Catholic Bishop who wished to stop conversions. A schoolmaster was threatened with death, and had to emigrate. A farmer was nearly killed. In another manufacturing parish, the Protestants were insulted, and got no redress. A Roman Catholic convert had to emigrate. A mother confessed on her death-bed that she had long been a Protestant, her daughter had to fly. This is English liberty!

the Rev. Mr. Campbell, a Wesleyan minister, which has just occurred at Athlone. Mr. Campbell's offence is that he preached the Gospel to Irish peasants anxious to hear it, and his treatment is, to be knocked down, maimed, and injured by miscreants set on him. If he wants further facts, let him call together, in any part of Ireland (I give him his choice), the teachers of the Irish Society, whose simple work is to teach the Irish peasant to read the Bible in his own language; and, when he finds from them that they have been set upon, bruised, and maimed by the priests' men, he will learn what instruments are used in Ireland to put down Protestant teaching.

<small>No liberty of conscience in Ireland.</small>

Mr. Bright talks of justice and righteousness. He quotes Scripture. Will he tell me if it is righteous or scriptural that Roman Catholics, who desire to read, and hear the story of the Gospel, should be brutally injured by a system of organized outrage? If he wants to do justice to Ireland, let him secure for millions, now oppressed, liberty to hear and read and think for themselves. This I assert, that there is no country in Europe, except Spain and the Roman States, in which at this moment, ay, and for the last fifty years, since the Irish Church began to be active, *liberty of conscience is so unknown as it is in Ireland.* Such is the organized

<small>Terror of Rome's law.</small>

tyranny in three provinces, that it is as much as a man's life is worth if he ventures to change his religion. Thousands have left the West of Ireland, within the last few years, because they were converts, and dared not remain. When the Rev. Mr. Mullen,* a Roman Catholic priest, complains that two millions of Irish emigrants, as soon as they arrive in the States, declare themselves Protestants, he shows us what is the detestable tyranny from which they have fled across the Atlantic. This I affirm, that hundreds of conversions to Protestantism are at this moment prevented, in three provinces in Ireland, by an organized system of terror, planned by Romish bishops, and carried out under their orders by the priests. When Mr. Fortescue talks about doing justice to Ireland, I tell him that if there ever were an honest Government, that had the courage to establish in Ireland the protection of English law, and to ensure safety of person, and security of trade, *whatever faith a man professes,* there would arise a secession from the Church of Rome, so large and general, in

---

* See his letter in the "Freeman's Journal," April 24, 1852.

Ireland, as to strike a panic into the Romish hierarchy. *This the priests know well, and they stop it by a reign of terror.*

When, therefore, Mr. Maguire complains of the words of an English lecturer, I meet him with this challenge: for every instance of coarse words used in England, I engage to produce ten instances of coarse deeds done in Ireland at the instigation of Rome. I will lay before the Lord Lieutenant (as he is a man of honour, who will not betray confidence) examples of brutal outrage, threatened or inflicted on Irish Romanists, whose only fault was that they disbelieved the fables of their Church and loathed the tyranny of their priests, but who knew well that, if they left the Romish, and joined the Protestant communion, their life would not be safe in Ireland, and their livelihood would be gone. I make this public challenge to these blustering orators, from Mr. Bright downwards to the Synans, Cogans, McEvoys, and O'Loghlens. They descant on justice to Ireland. I shall believe them to be honest, when they have grappled with this foul injustice, contrary to English liberty, and to every principle of reason and Scripture. When they have liberated the Irish peasant from an oppression the most degrading that has ever prevailed in Europe, then we shall reckon them friends of justice and righteousness.

<small>Offer to Rome's orator and Mr. Bright.</small>

The experience of our Irish Church Missions, which now extends over twenty years, is on this question decisive. Whenever in the south or west of Ireland our missionaries have ventured to preach and teach, they have met always one treatment—curiosity, attention, kindness among the people; from the myrmidons of the priests—brickbats, bludgeons, and blows. They have (by the assistance given them by a resolute English society) been enabled to hold their ground, and the result has been that this organized conspiracy against liberty has been baffled, and the popular desire to hear and read has remained. In Galway, in Tuam, and Clifden, even in Limerick, the Roman Catholic people have become the friends of the Protestant missionary, and, receiving him at first with distrust, have welcomed him at last with affectionate regard.*

<small>Irish Church Missions.</small>

---

* The allusion in the "Quarterly Review" (No. 249, p. 261) to the evils of proselytizing is not creditable to its author. When he says that " it has always proved the surest enemy to peace and goodwill in Ireland," I answer, that the writer had better ask the present Bishop of Tuam, or the nephew of the late Bishop, or the clergymen of Clifden or Tuam, and he will learn that the reverse is the fact. If controversy is conducted in a Christian spirit, it always leads, as it has led in hundreds of cases, to peace and goodwill.

Rome silences discussion.

But on Mr. Maguire's plan, all possibility of such action and all preaching would cease. For, as Protestant preaching is always met by priestly outrage, the outrage of the mob would be adduced as a reason why the preaching should be put down. It would then be only necessary, in Wigan, or Limerick, or Manchester, for the priest to summon his agents, a brutal mob would stop the preacher, and close the lecture.* Magistrates, mayors, and police would then become the priests' accomplices, and, as they would declare that a breach of the peace was imminent, all preaching and discussion would cease in England and Ireland. This is the aim of Rome. Is it the purpose of England?

The magistrates of Belfast last winter put a stop to a lecturer, and drove him from the town. Now the magistrates at Bolton, and at Manchester, have interdicted Mr. Murphy. The priests and their mobs attempted some years ago to close our schools in Dublin. The police stood aloof and left our teachers and children to the brickbats of the mob. Happily at that time Lord Palmerston was living, and Lord Palmerston, unlike Mr. Gladstone, was an Englishman who loved liberty. To him we resorted; at his orders the police did their duty, and the violence ceased. Thousands of ignorant, neglected children, taught in the schools which the priests tried to close, have had occasion to bless his name.

Queenstown Case. Outrages.

Two recent cases will further illustrate the system. Dr. Collis lives at Queenstown, in county Cork. The neighbourhood is, of course, Roman Catholic. But among that rude people there are tastes, and a growing desire for inquiry. Dr. Collis opened a shop for the sale of Bibles. No one could have a Bible without purchase; all might have the Bible who would buy—an offer, one would think, so inoffensive that even priestly tyranny might have borne it. But no; the shop was resorted to freely; therefore it was a nuisance. At all risks it must be closed. A Protestant had let the premises to Dr. Collis. He was threatened, and the lease was given up. But Dr. Collis got new premises on a twenty-one years' lease. Therefore more vigorous measures must be employed.

The Canon Laws enforced.

The priest first tried the authorities; he followed the plan of Messrs. Rearden and Maguire. He appealed to the gentry; he applied to the bench of magistrates; he went to the Commissioners of police. They should interfere to put down this nuisance—a sale of Bibles in a Roman Catholic country!—intolerable!

* This has already begun against Mr. Murphy in Bolton and in Manchester: more illegal proceedings have hardly ever been perpetrated.

But Irish magistrates and police shrink at present from the application of the Canon Law; they refused to interfere. But Queenstown abounds in Fenians, and Fenians (as we have learnt at Manchester and Clerkenwell) employ short, sharp modes of procedure. So the priest took the matter into his own hands, and denounced the sale of Bibles from the altar. Soon after Dr. Collis received a notice to prepare his coffin.

In the county of Louth the Redemptorists, last winter, announced a mission. Nothing is more reasonable. The Roman Catholic Church often employs these itinerant agencies with effect. But Ireland is under British law, and what is open to the Roman priest is open to the Protestant pastor. A clergyman anticipated the Redemptorists, and delivered lectures, and, as these were both stringent and largely attended, the Redemptorists fled from the field. But from the altar the priest issued his curse against the preacher, and a curse is not meant to be harmless. Louth Case.

Can any man doubt what will be the result when, in Ireland, magistrates, mayors, and police commissioners, guided by a Romish Lord Chancellor and a Romish Lord Lieutenant, exert against the teaching of Protestants their coercive power. To speak of the progress of Protestantism in Ireland under such a system is a mockery. Protestantism will disappear from three provinces in Ireland. It would be a cruel folly to expose to such treatment the lives of earnest missionaries. Only since Napoleon's reign have Protestants been able to preach and teach in France. It is only possible now through the strong will of a resolute man. Weak Lord Lieutenants, timid Irish Secretaries, treacherous Under-secretaries, will become the tools of Dr. Cullen, and the agents of his plans. In Ulster alone will Protestantism survive, and there only through organized force, probably in the end through a fierce civil war; and then I suspect England (if at least she is ruled by Messrs. Gladstone and Bright) will be found denouncing the Irish Protestants, and abetting the Romish priests, leagued with England's bitterest enemies, and crushing by her bayonets her only remaining friends. Suppression Protestant preaching in Ireland.

But the effects will also be felt in England. Then some future Mr. Rearden will put more skilfully his questions, and an English Home Secretary will rise and ask leave to bring in a Bill to prevent all controversial lectures* except in churches during Divine service, and then only after having passed the censorship of the Home Office,

* This was Mr. Rearden's proposal.

not without the advice of Dr. Manning. Then the future Premier will direct his declamation against the evils of religious strife, and the hateful passions of polemical warfare; he will prove that the way to have peace in Ireland is to leave the population serfs of the Romish bishops, and to introduce into England the salutary law of Turkey, that no one shall either write, or preach, or speak against that ancient faith held by so many millions, and endeared by centuries of tradition to so many faithful hearts.

The future of the Liberationists.

Then the Nonconformists will see in its true light the bearings of their recent treaty with Dr. Cullen. Great will be the chuckling of the Romish hierarchy when they turn their hands on their present accomplices, and crush them under their feet as worthless tools. Dissenters will then learn how wise were the words of a Baptist minister who knew Ireland well, and who thus describes events that are near:—

"I am fully convinced that liberty of conscience in this country (Ireland) will not long survive the demolition of the Establishment. Whatever demagogues may say, I have no notion that our political Reformers have any such blindness of view as that, if our Establishment were put down, another would not take its place. Such a hope may be held out to quell unwary Dissenters, but it can deceive no man acquainted with the history and genius of Popery."*

The dreams of the Liberation Society are in truth, ni respect of Ireland, the veriest chimeras; they are laying deep and broad the foundations of the ascendency of Rome. Its wealth will be abundant. Mr. Gladstone will start it with four millions and a half, and this but the beginning. Mines of gold await the hierarchy, richer than in the United States; for in New York the Protestants form only five-sixths of the population, yet the hierarchy extort vast sums.† In Ireland Rome commands three-fourths of the population: what limit is there to her acquisition of wealth and power? If anyone will read the picture of Newfoundland, as given before a Committee of the House of Com-

---

* Rev. Dr. Carson's Letter to Lord Plunket. Works, vol. ii., p. 188.

† "There is no limit to the demands which the Romanists are making on the public purse. In New York they control the Treasury, and, by their men in the Common Council, vote to their sectarian Institutions thousands of the people's money every year. They go also to the State Legislature, and unblushingly ask for such a list of appropriations as this. We copy from the Assembly Bill, No. 606, entitled an 'Act making Appropriations for Charitable

mons in 1841,* they will discover what the Romish priests can do with a subservient Parliament.

and Public Purposes,' which includes, among numerous gifts to hospitals, asylums, and other charities, the following among other items, relating particularly to New York and Brooklyn, to wit:—

	Dollars.
For the Church of St. Mary, in the city of New York, to aid in maintenance of schools under its charge	5,000
For the Church of St. Bridget, ditto	5,000
,, St. Vincent, ditto	1,000
,, Transfiguration, ditto	5,000
,, Immaculate Conception, ditto	5,000
,, St. Patrick, ditto	5,000
For the School of the Church of our Lady of the Angels	3,000
For the Church of St. Joseph, in Brooklyn, to aid in the maintenance of schools under its charge	3,000
For the Sisters of Mercy, in Brooklyn, ditto.	5,000
,, Church of St. Peter, New York, ditto	3,000
,, St. Lawrence School, in New York	5,000
For the Church of St. James's, New York, to aid in the maintenance of schools under its charge	3,000
For the Church of St. Paul, New York, ditto	2,500
,, St. Joseph ,, ,,	1,000
,, St. Stephen ,, ,,	2,000
,, St. Gabriel ,, ,,	3,000
,, St. Michael ,, ,,	3,000
,, St. Nicholas ,, ,,	2,000
,, St. Theresa ,, ,,	3,000
,, St. Rosa ,, ,,	3,000

The late New York Legislature, the most corrupt and infamous in all the annals of the State, made a high bid for the Irish and Catholic vote, in appropriating not less than 77,000 dols. to Catholic institutions, against 54,000 dols. to Protestant Establishments, notwithstanding that the population of the States is three-fourths, if not five-sixths, Protestant. As the donations passed the Democratic House, and before they reached the Republican Senate, where they were cut down and their proportions changed, 242,736 dols. were given to Catholic Establishments, and 131,480 dols. to Protestants.

* It would be well if that evidence could be printed. It would prepare us for what is coming. The Bishop and priests returned the members, sat under the gallery, overawed the House (I commend the example to Dr. Manning) —no one could dare to vote or even take in a newspaper without consulting his priest. People say ignorantly, what need we care for Rome's Canon Law? Look at the elections now in Ireland. The bishops and priests meet and nominate the members, and if any one hesitates to vote for them he is ruined, and will have his head broken. For Mr. Gladstone and the Romish members having secured a small number of polling booths, no man can give his vote against the priests without hazard of his life. This is English liberty! But this is the carrying out of the Canon Law.

CHAPTER III.

PROGRESS OF THE CHURCH OF ROME IN ENGLAND FROM 1829 TO 1846.

Repeal movement. WE turn now to trace the progress of the Romish hierarchy from its first possession of Parliamentary power in 1829. For many years after that period Mr. O'Connell was the agent of the Church of Rome. The priests returned the members who formed what was popularly called O'Connell's tail, and they collected the rent which paid the expenses of the elections and the agency. The party amounted to above thirty. By the skilful use of this number, by threatening and alarming the Whig Cabinet, they constrained the Government to defer to their plans. As soon as the Romish Bishops felt their strength, they set on foot two movements; the one was directed against the Irish Church, which was obnoxious to the peasants, through the payment of tithe and cess—burdens which fell on the tenant farmers. In this agitation they sought and obtained the assistance of the English voluntaries, who were then beginning to be active, but were more noisy than strong. A change in the tithe and cess was introduced by the Government, which transferred these from the farmer tenants to the Irish landlords; this change allayed the storm, and it could not be revived. But there was another movement, far more popular, into which the passionate sentiment of the Irish people and of the priests drove the agitator reluctantly. He was compelled to unfurl the green standard, to raise the cry of independence, and to demand the repeal of the Union. He was aware how hopeless such a demand was, but the cry was too strong for him.* The priests and people hated England as they do now,

---

* Ignorant men trace Fenianism to temporary causes or foreign influence. It is merely the outbreak of deep-seated hatred. Read the oath which prevailed in Kerry, &c., in 1858:—"I do solemnly swear that I renounce all allegiance to the Queen of England, that I will do all that may be in my power to make Ireland an independent democratic republic, that I will implicitly obey all the orders of my superiors, and will take up arms at the first summons."—*Senior*, ii., 86.

and sought separation. For the hatred of the Sassenach and of the English conqueror has been kept up by the influence of the priests in the Irish mind as fresh to our times, as in the rebellion of 1641, the war of 1688, and the insurrection of 1798. Hence the cry of Repeal, in which the priests were the agents, ran as a war cry over Ireland. When on the hill of Tara O'Connell met an enormous multitude, and was presented with a crown, a look or a nod from him would have raised a rebellion. Mr. Wyse tells us in his history how near that was in 1828. "When will he call us out?" was whispered by thousands.* The feeling was as universal in 1842 and 3. It needed all the great demagogue's power to prevent a national rising.

This was the second step of the Romish priesthood. They sprang, like leopards from their ambush, on the bewildered English; dropping disguise, aiming at their real object, the separation of Ireland from England, they thought that at last the time was come when, with an army of their own, and a Government obeying their will, they might (through a Parliament like that under James II.) expel the Sassenach, and crush by force the heretic. {.sidenote Parliamentary Tactics of Rome.}

Then they would settle the land question more promptly than Messrs. Bright and Mill; the Fitzwilliams, Lansdownes, Cavendishs, and Beresfords would soon be dealt with; the land would be adjusted to meet their claims and the demands of the Church of Rome; for these, Bishop Moriarty tells us, can never be withdrawn. But these prospects so bright, these sanguine hopes, were abruptly closed by the Irish famine. Then the population sank with a fearful collapse. Death and exile swept away millions, and left those, on whom the priests depended, reduced in numbers and prostrate in spirit for many years.

Yet, even in this unlooked-for reverse, the Romish hierarchy never relaxed their efforts, or lost sight of their aim. It was plain to them that the prospect of Repeal must be postponed for some years. Smith O'Brien was a poor counterpart of O'Connell, and the cabbage-garden rising was a wretched substitute for the hill of Tara. But on a quieter arena, in a different scene, they found scope enough for their energies. They concentrated their attention on England. There much might be done to advance their future plans.

The English Government had at that moment passed from the weakened hands of the Whigs into the hands of an able and

* See Wyse's "History of the Catholic Association."

experienced statesman. If the Irish Bishops could deceive Sir Robert Peel, their objects might be gained. They presented to him a captivating plea. They appealed to him in the meekest accents, and in the humblest attitude. They were poor, suffering men, desiring education for their students, but unable from poverty to supply it—their college walls crumbling in decay, their admirable professors starving, their disciples pigging two in a bed in virtuous poverty—and besides all this, their own feelings, so keenly sensitive, were exposed to continual vexation. For the grant to Maynooth, as it appeared on the yearly estimate, led to a recurrence of bitter attacks by Protestant bigots, who used the occasion to lacerate the feelings of a large but impoverished community. Only make the grant to Maynooth permanent, and this trial would cease; increase it, and their poverty would be relieved. And then their gratitude! how lasting! What a reward for a popular statesman! Do this, and Sir Robert Peel would despatch a message of peace to Ireland; and Ireland, satisfied and thankful, would henceforth repose in the arms of the great statesman in lasting regard. This pleasant epic, carried by the Romish Bishops to the Lord-Lieutenant, and through him presented to Sir James Graham and Sir Robert Peel, had the full effect of an attractive romance. It charmed the Government, and it deceived them. We need hardly say that the statements of distress were fictions. When they had served their turn, the story of decaying walls and double-bedded students was laughed at. But the fiction served its turn; it deceived the Premier, it deluded the House of Commons, and, in spite of the resistance of the British People, the blunder of the Maynooth Endowment Act was forced on the country.

The romance. 1845.

But no sooner was this accomplished than the dissolving view of peace faded away. Instead of gratitude there was grievance, and, before the Act was dry on the Statute Book, the old cry of oppression was ringing loud and strong through Ireland. In another twelvemonth, the Romish Bishops, backed by the priests, were howling vehemently at the door of Parliament. But, while pleas of distress brought them to Parliament as beggars, they were active in advancing their deep-laid plans. The folly of Parliament had just enabled them to educate their students at the public expense. It gave them a large yearly grant, and left them to prosecute more easily their schemes of ambition. In 1846, before the stir of Maynooth was allayed, they started two projects, which were to open, through Parliament, new avenues to power.

The reality.

One project was brought forward in the House of Commons by an English barrister, a Protestant, not apparently connected with the Church of Rome. If I remember right, Mr. Watson sat for an Irish borough. At all events, he was a compliant agent of the Romish Bishops, whose instructions he obeyed. O'Connell was then in his decay, and it was wise to place in less suspected hands the work of the Romish hierarchy. What those plans were may be best stated in the words of the eminent statesman Sir James Graham, who, when Home Secretary, had to discuss them. "The present Bill," he says, in 1846, "consists of four enactments;" and he describes them thus : The first enables the Archbishops and Bishops of the Roman Catholic Church to assume the title of the sees of the Protestant Church; the second sanctions the appearance of Roman Catholic prelates and priests in pontificals in public places; the third allows a judge, mayor, or sheriff to attend mass in his robes of office; and the fourth removes all restrictions on the Regular orders, so as to allow the country to be filled with Jesuits and monks. These proposals, urged within a twelvemonth of the grant to Maynooth, by the same Bishops who had vowed to the minister their eternal gratitude, illustrated the value of the promises and pledges of the Romish hierarchy. Sir James Graham and Sir Robert Peel resisted these proposals, but the House, perplexed and deceived, adopted them. Mr. Watson's Bill fell through in consequence of the events of that eventful year. It is only worthy of notice now, as it shows how clearly Rome chooses her objects, and with what tenacity, like a bloodhound, she pursues them.

Mr. Watson's Bills. 1846.

While this project was set on foot by the grateful prelates in the House of Commons, another mine was sprung by them in the House of Lords. In all foreign countries no Bull from the Pope can be sent to Romish Bishops and received as of authority, till it has been submitted to the Government and had its sanction. Nor is this precaution surprising, for a Papal Bull, as it may relieve subjects from their allegiance and may declare the title of a Sovereign forfeited, is rather a serious affair for a Monarchy. Long before the Reformation, England had adopted this precaution. By the Act of Edward I.* to publish a Bull of excommunication against any one subjected parties to the penalty of treason. By the statute of Richard II., the introduction and publication of any bull directed against the Sovereign or Government, for any political purpose,

Bill in the House of Lords. 1846.

---

* Lord Lyndhurst, May 11, 1846, Hansard, p. 316, 17.

subjected the parties to the penalties of a *premunire*. This precaution appeared so necessary, and the claim of the Popes to supreme authority was felt to be so intolerable, that Lord Lyndhurst said, and Lord Brougham concurred, "If any person improperly, wantonly, or seditiously called in question the supremacy of the Crown of England (and that, it was to be observed, included the temporal as well as the spiritual power of the Crown), . . . that person would be liable to prosecution at Common Law."

<small>Lord Lyndhurst's Bill.</small>

Other remarks made by this eminent jurist are well deserving of remembrance, now that we see a little more of the developed designs of the Church of Rome. That Church, he said, never retraced its steps, never abandoned its course; its canons never varied; the power of deposing monarchs and absolving subjects* from allegiance, formed a portion of them; and every priest, whether regular or secular, swore to obey those laws; facts, as he remarked, well·" calculated to excite our indignation."

But Lord Lyndhurst thought that the common law was strong enough to protect England from Romish encroachments, and to put down any Bull or decree of the Pope, directed either against the Crown, or an individual. Under this impression Lord Lyndhurst, on the part of Government, consented to withdraw the prohibition on the Papacy, and to allow free access for any communication from the Pope to the Romish hierarchy in England; and the House of Lords was guided by his high authority.

<small>Claims of Rome.</small>

The use, however, to which the Romish bishops turned this permission, was not clearly understood till the inquiry last year, before a Committee of the House of Commons on the Ecclesiastical Titles Act, brought out the real objects of Rome, and the uses to which she applied the change in our laws. It then appeared, on the evidence of the Romish Bishops themselves, what a stride the Romish hierarchy had made to open defiance of English law. It was frankly stated by Bishop Moriarty (who has been styled a moderate ecclesiastic!!) and by Mr. Hope Scott, who, an able bar-

---

* See Petition of Rev. R. J. McGhee, presented to the House of Commons in July, 1868, by Mr. Gladstone. Six Bulls, or Papal Laws, are now in full force, of which Dr. Doyle said of one of them, that, *if it was in force, nothing in England would be at rest or in peace.* It is our own wilful blindness not to know what Rome holds as her laws, which, as Lord Lyndhurst says, are unalterable. The letters of Sir G. Bowyer are really too flimsy to deserve an answer, and, after his exposure by Dr. Cumming, his facts may be treated as barefaced fictions. See also the able letters of Dr. M'Neile in the *Times* of August last.

…ister, was sure to give a guarded exposition of the claims of his Church, that the Romish Bishops disregard the authority of Parliament, and, if any law passed by Parliament comes into conflict with a law of the Pope, the latter only is binding on their conscience and conduct.*

So that we have admitted into the English Parliament a band of men, who take an active part in framing or altering our laws, but who consider our policy only of importance as it affects the higher policy of the Roman State, and whose single object it is to bend our laws so as to make them conform to the canons of the Papacy, and to promote the system of ecclesiastical power, a system which keeps a people ignorant in order that priests may reign.† {Parliamentary action of Rome.}

Hence these witnesses lay it down with a naïveté, which is truly instructive, that if our Parliament passes at any time a law which interferes with the statutes of the Church of Rome, that law is null and void, and is treated by them with contempt. And they carry out this principle, so frankly avowed, with perfect consistency. For if the foreign policy of England happens to be adverse to the interests of that miserable State, over which the Pope rules, there rises a yell of rebellion from the Romish priests against our Queen. And their organs in the public press faithfully reflect this bold disloyalty. {Romish "loyalty," what it is.}

I take an extract from the "Times," which has lately praised Bishop Moriarty. Here is its comment, in 1859, on the words of this moderate bishop :—

* This is clearly avowed in the *Univers*, the great Roman Catholic organ. It says, March, 28, 1868 :—" In this country we cannot, as Catholics, attach ourselves permanently to any political party until we have such perfect religious equality as will allow us to hope that a Catholic may aspire to the high office of Prime Minister of England. No party tie, no supposed debt of gratitude, can relieve him of that duty to his country and his Church. A Catholic should never attach himself to any political party composed mainly of heretics. No one who is truly at heart a thorough and complete Catholic can give his entire adhesion to a Protestant leader, be he Whig or Tory, for in so doing he divides the allegiance—in some instances destroys it altogether—which he owes to the Church. A Catholic cannot give himself up to any party in a Protestant country."

† Ecclesiastical Titles Committee; See Hope Scott, p. 460-1-3-4-5, 525, 559; Bp. Moriarty, 789-90, 661. Bishop Moriarty puts the case plainly in his evidence before the Maynooth Commissioners. In every temporal matter which touches religion (and all do), "the direction concerning them appertains to the Church, which is the authorised exponent of the law of God on earth, and therefore to the Pope."—Maynooth Commission, vol. ii. page 128. See also pp. 130, 1.

"Let any one read the speech of Dr. Moriarty at Killarney, or the disgraceful scene which occurred at the Meeting in Cork, and then ask himself whether such things are the result of British institutions, and whether he can recognise in them any one of those characteristics which, in spite of all their political differences, distinguish Englishmen from the rest of mankind. *Where but in a Roman Catholic meeting, presided over by a bishop and harangued by deans and canons,* could the name of the Queen be received with a burst of disapprobation, which rendered the speaker inaudible, from the very voices which yelled out a determination to fight for the Pope?

<small>Rome's defiance of our Sovereign.</small>

"From whom *but a Roman Catholic bishop* could one hear it laid down, that it was the duty of a constituency in these islands to exercise their influence on their representatives in order to induce the Government of this country *to put down a rebellion in a foreign State, not on any ground of public policy, in which the interests of England are concerned,* but only because that tyrannical sovereign was the head of their Church, and they had, therefore, a vested interest in perpetuating his tyranny and corruption. *There is no divided allegiance, as was apprehended. This allegiance is wholly given to one person,* and nothing is left for the Queen but yells of disapprobation and the accusation of having starved two millions of her subjects."—"Times," 1859.

Every one will remember the shouts of exultation in the Romish press in Ireland at our disasters in India, and our difficulties in the Crimea,* gloating over these as signs that the sun of England was obscured, and that our downfall was near; and not less remarkable was it to see, while England and Scotland mourned their lost Prince, that Irish caricatures held him up to public scorn, and, when the Prince of Wales was married, amidst a nation's rejoicing, the Romish press inspired by priests, and Romish students taught by priests, openly expressed their indifference and antipathy.

But this habitual disloyalty shows itself on all suitable occasions, and puts forward the insolent claim that a Romish priest shall be above our laws.

<small>Rome's defiance of the laws of England.</small>

(1) The laws of England, with a just abhorrence of crime, enact that any person knowing and concealing a crime shall

* Senior, "Journals," ii., 113, 1858:—"Disaffection to the English Government is as deep and as wide as it ever was. The mass of the people sympathized with the French, with the Americans, with the Russians, even with the Sepoys. During the Crimean war, though more than half of our troops were Irishmen, the popular newspapers delighted in exaggerating all our losses, and in praising the Russians and French to our disadvantage. The anti-English feeling is such that no one who has held office has any chance with a popular Irish constituency."

be treated as an accomplice. But a Roman priest refuses to declare the crime, on the plea * that his Church empowers him to receive confession, and directs him not to divulge it.

(2) Our law requires that on any reasonable suspicion that a person is illegally confined, a writ shall issue, and, at the demand of the officer of the law, the doors of the prison shall fly open, and the captive shall be brought before the Court. But there are many places in England and Ireland in which women are held in restraint contrary to their will, and, because they are called convents, English law is defied, and the helpless are immured.

(3) It is the boast of England that as soon as a slave touches our soil he is free, yet children and women are† seized by the agents of the Church of Rome, muffled, bound, dragged abroad, and thrust into Romish prisons, where neither parents nor relatives are suffered to approach them, because they are called convents, or monastic institutions.

(4) Our Legislature enacts that the Executive Government shall enter, inspect, and examine every school which receives public aid. But the Romish bishops refuse to admit to their schools or their reformatories any one except those whom they are pleased to recognise as their agents, and who, in fact, are their accomplices.

So true is the remark of Dr. Manning, that the struggle between the supremacy of our Sovereign and the supremacy of the Pope

---

* I annex this as a just mode of dealing with such men:—A ROMAN CATHOLIC PRIEST COMMITTED TO PRISON.—A negro was lynched in Frankfort, Kentucky, in January last, who, it is alleged, had committed an outrage on an Irish girl, and afterwards attempted to murder her. One of the witnesses, the Rev. Lambert Young, a Roman Catholic priest, declined to give his testimony before the grand jury, and appealed to the United States Court. The question was whether he knew the persons who broke into the gaol, in which he was present when the mob took out the prisoner. The Court held that the communications were not privileged, and that while Mr. Young might think that, by answering the questions, he would degrade himself in the estimation of the clergy of which he was a member, and would probably lose his influence with his congregation, still the interest of the State ought not to suffer by the policy of any individual. Mr. Young, however, persisted in refusing, whereupon he was adjudged to be in contempt, and *was ordered to be committed to prison until he answered the questions.*

† The scandalous case of the poor girl dragged to Dover, and thence across the Channel, will be in the recollection of all. She was called a maniac. Is a poor creature, driven mad by cruelty in a convent, not to be under the protection of our law?

is a struggle for life and death, and embraces the whole question of the Reformation. Far more, it is the old battle fought under the Plantagenets, whether the law of England is to be sovereign and supreme, or whether we are to have a confederacy of Roman priests, aided by treacherous English priests, braving English law, defying the British Parliament,* and trampling on the Sovereign's Crown.†

---

* "I do not think that the people like the priests more than they did, but they fear them more, . . . now Archbishop Cullen is converting the Church into a monarchy, with the Pope for its king, and himself for its viceroy."—Senior, ii., 114.

† Mr. Gladstone derided the statement of Mr. Disraeli, that there was a combination of Ritualists with Romanists against our institutions.

(1.) If Mr. Gladstone will read Dr. Lee's letter addressed to Mr. Hardy,‡ just published (pp. 5, 6, 7, 8), he will find that Dr. Lee and his friends hold that nothing but *our subjection to the Pope* (whom he styles the " Primate of Christendom ") will enable us to make head against the evils of our day. The "primacy of the central see" is the only salvation "for the Church and the soul." Is that no alliance with Rome? Does he want more proof, let him add to Dr. Lee, Dr. Littledale (" Innovations: a Lecture"), and he will find the attacks on the Reformation and on the Reformers, which have been uttered for three centuries by the most scurrilous of the Popish writers, repeated by these Ritualists.

(2.) Let him turn to three thick volumes, edited by Mr. Orby Shipley, and if he can find in the Roman catalogue of books any grosser statements of Roman dogmas and fables, I shall be surprised. Yet these views are held and taught *by clergy professing to be members of the Church of England.*

(3.) Let him listen to his friend Dr. Pusey, who tells the Church Union that he is in close communication with Romish Bishops on the terms of union with Rome, which he thinks easy.

(4.) Does he want more evidence? Has he never read the newspapers of that party, or noticed the secessions of the more honest to Rome? a whole sisterhood, this spring, announced to the Convocation by the Bishop of London; the curate of the notorious Mr. Skinner has just joined Rome.

(5.) Is more wanted? What does he think of clergymen, holding our benefices, whose wives are Papists (and therefore in constant communication with Romish priests), and who, professing to be Anglican clergy, send their daughters to be immured as nuns in Romish convents? Is that no alliance with Rome? The time is near when we may have to make further revelations, and to show that there are hundreds of English clergymen, in secret connivance with the Church of Rome, while they eat, to our injury and their shame, the bread of our Reformed Church.

‡ The Church of England and Political Parties. By the Rev. F. G. Lee. (Bosworth, Regent-street.)

CHAPTER IV.

THE PROGRESS OF ROME FROM 1846 TO 1864.

Up to the year 1846, when the Conservative ministry was overthrown, there had been a steady progress in the Romish advance in Parliament. When Rome was debarred from a rising in Ireland by the decline of population and the pressure of famine, the Romish hierarchy wisely used the interval to plant in the minds of statesmen and of the House of Commons those germs of opinion which were soon to be developed into action. Through the deception practised on Sir Robert Peel, and the plausible assertion of new grievances, the hierarchy had, till the middle of 1846, when Lord John Russell returned to power, made a steady progress. *Fall of Conservatism.*

But here there was a pause. Foreign affairs engrossed the attention of Lord Palmerston, the ablest member of the new Government. The course of foreign policy plunged the Whig Government into strong antagonism to the Papal party. The Pope and his cause were united with Austria, Spain, and the bigoted Governments of Naples and Tuscany. Lord Palmerston and the Liberal Government were regarded by Belgium and France as the natural leaders of a more liberal and tolerant system.

The Romish Prelates cannot succeed in Parliament, except when the opposite parties in politics are nearly balanced, and require the votes of the Irish band. Then, indeed, by throwing their weight into the scale, they adjust the balance and can claim their price. But in 1846, and for several years after, the Conservative party was depressed and shattered. The Liberals had an overwhelming preponderance in Parliament. Nor with the Liberal party, as then constituted, did the Romish priests find favour; in truth, the Romish newspapers abused and reviled the Whigs. Mr. Gladstone's sympathies with Italy, expressed in his letter to Lord Aberdeen, threw him far adrift from Romish moorings. These were long, dark days for the hierarchy, and they lasted, with little sunshine, for nearly twenty years. But the Papacy can afford to wait; its schemes *1847. Dark days for Rome.*

seldom fail, and its sagacity is seldom at fault. Popes become dull, incapable, and lethargic, but the cabinet of the Vatican is always effective. It contains the united intellect of Europe and of the New World, the subtilty of the Italian, the acuteness of the Frenchman, the perseverance of the German, the American's boisterous elasticity, and the duplicity of Oriental craft. That cabinet has, like the Russian, the advantage of an agency carefully prepared, nurtured from early youth, trained in diplomacy, scattered over all parts of the world, deriving from every court and capital experience and information, and transmitting their intelligence to one central office. To Rome also, once in three years, every bishop from every part of the world repairs, and reports himself to the Roman Inquisition; pouring into its watchful ear his statements and impressions. Such a cabinet is never uninformed, and it rarely makes a blunder.

Papal Aggression of 1851.

Apparently it had made a mistake in its movement on England in 1851. The germ of that movement we observed in Mr. Watson's Bill in 1846. The Roman bishops then laid their fingers quietly on the pulses of the House of Commons. But Sir James Graham's speech warned them that the patient was not reduced to the desired weakness. They behoved to wait. When they moved five years later, there was a division in the Papal cabinet; a section was opposed to the aggression. But Dr. Wiseman was confident, and his authority prevailed. His advice was taken, and the *bold claim was put forward (a claim bolder than had been ventured on since the days of Richard II.) that the Pope should usurp the Queen's prerogative, and parcel out England into dioceses at his pleasure. It was a daring act, which the Norman, the Plantagenet, and the Tudor would have instantly put down. But Dr. Wiseman judged correctly of the collapse of English sentiment, and the growing indifference to the rights of the Sovereign and the duties of Parliament. The aggression, indeed, produced at the moment a strong excitement; it made the heart of the nation beat high. There was a burst of national emotion, but emotion exhausts itself, and a crafty enemy can always wait for the recoil. The sight of a fox rouses the

Its real import.

---

* Petty reasoners, like Sir G. Bowyer, cavil and quibble. The "Univers," the Romish organ, states the case plainly:—"We prefer, since the Holy See has thought fit to take this grave step, to avow plainly and openly its bearing. Yes, the Act of Supremacy just exercised by Pius IX., *denies the existence in England of all other spiritual authority save his own.*"

cries of the poultry-yard, but, if the intruder waits and comes again, he may pounce on his victim. So Rome bowed her head, and, when the excitement had passed, she came back and seized her prey. Even during the interval, when it was necessary to be still, she had useful works to occupy her. Dr. Cullen * had arrived in Ireland, and stepped into the post once filled by Dr. Troy and Dr. Murray, but he held it under different circumstances. These prelates had lived when Rome was weak. Dr. Cullen arrived when the Church was strong. He pursued therefore an altered policy. Formerly the weapon was craft and intreaty; now it was threats and force. He came, as Legate, with overwhelming power; he set up the authority of the Roman cabinet, and made the Irish bishops bend to his will. A new system was introduced. Implicit obedience to the Papal cabinet was enforced. Weakness and timidity had before this time made concessions: the National Schools had been recognised, the Secular Colleges had been allowed to spread. All this must be changed —no more concessions, no further compromises—but the stern, unsparing demands of Rome. The Secular Colleges were denounced; a college under the Bishops' sole authority was set up. No priest was suffered to give religious instruction in the Secular colleges, and, deprived of religious instruction, they were denounced as profane. Dr. Newman had been sent for to preside over Dr. Cullen's college, but Dr. Newman's genius and spirit were incompatible with Romish tyranny; he was driven away. The National Schools were denounced. What folly to suffer schools to exist which taught the peasants to read and think for themselves! The Irish Government was eagerly pressed: modifications in the Board were demanded, and the demand was complied with. First, Bible extracts and liberal books disappeared; on this ground Archbishop Whately left the Board in disgust. Secondly, bigoted Commissioners were added; this was done by Mr. Cardwell. Thirdly, the rules were revised and altered; the training school was especially objected to. Its superior discipline was odious to the priests. Nuns and monks were employed to train teachers as ignorant as themselves. But these concessions were not sufficient, they only whetted the appetite for more. The more abject the tone of the Government, the bolder and more exacting Dr. Cullen grew. At last a demand came, loud, clear, and peremptory: "Pay us the money, and leave

Dr. Cullen.

New Romish tactics.

* He was appointed by the Roman cabinet against the wish of the Irish Bishops.

to us the schools,"—so boldly, with colours flying, did Dr. Cullen march on his way to power.

But while Rome was thus advancing in Ireland, events, that occurred in England, threw open a still more important field. The Church of Rome in Ireland, by the appointment of Dr. Cullen as Legate, had acquired unity of purpose and firmness of aim. Dr. Cullen kept his priests in order: the contumacious were subdued. Even Archbishop McHale had to bow his head and obey. Archbishop Leahy has revealed to a Committee* how complete was the subjugation of the Irish Bishops and Priests to the orders of Rome. The *mot d'ordre* was given by Dr. Cullen, and was obeyed. Archbishop Leahy had supported the National Board. In forty-six parishes he had set up, in each, one to eight National Schools. One of the Commissioners, Mr. Waldron, had been his intimate friend, and had owed his seat in Parliament to his support. But at the election in 1865, all this was changed; the Archbishops, Bishops, and Priests turned right round and denounced the National Board which they had once supported. Mr. Waldron was cashiered, and a Captain White was pitchforked into the county of Tipperary.† The mode of election, Archbishop Leahy tells us, was in this wise. He sent for all his priests to his house; they met in conclave; and settled who was to be the member. The minority agreed to follow the majority, and the whole black regiment moved with edifying unanimity. Sundays and the chapels were the choice occasions for their political canvass—not in the chapel, says the Archbishop, that would be profane; but in the chapel-yard, before the congregation disperses, for that is right and holy! The duty of returning members is sacred, it concerns spiritual functions; the Priest must exhort his people that it is as much as their souls are worth if they vote for Mr. Waldron, and don't vote for Captain White. So all through Ireland, at the nod of the Cardinal, sixty members were returned to Parliament, sworn champions of the Church of Rome. Old Sarum or Gatton never showed so edifying a unity.

Now the time had come when the struggle of political parties was resumed, and Dr. Cullen could make his hand felt by both. The Conservatives, once broken, had rallied; for a short time

---

* See "Committee on Tipperary Election," p. 34.

† The same course is pursued this month by Dr. McHale and his priests meeting at Castlebar, County Mayo.—*Freeman's Journal*, August 8, 1868. But this is only a specimen of the practice pursued throughout Ireland Romish Bishop names every Member of county and borough in Ireland.

they had risen to office. The Liberals were disunited, and, through their division, the Conservatives might rise again. It was worth while for Dr. Cullen to look to both sides, and to act upon both. So the word was given, and the pressure was felt in England as well as Ireland. In some of the English boroughs the Roman Catholic voters voted for the Conservatives; in one of the Irish counties, the priests returned a Conservative. That gentleman sat on the bench of Opposition, received circulars and dined with Mr. Disraeli. The London organs of the Romish party favoured the Conservative side, and contrasted their foreign policy with the Italian policy of the Liberals. *Influence in English elections.*

In England at this time the Romish Church had undergone an important change. One of the modern perverts had been noticed for his ability. His acuteness, dexterity, and address were observed; he had been distinguished in the Church of England by eminent qualifications. When he joined the Church of Rome, his prostration of intellect to the will of the Pope, showed an edifying obedience. There was no fable, however gross, that he did not swallow, if his Church declared it; there was no outrage on reason or morals which staggered him, if only his Church propounded it. Such a recruit was invaluable. He had none of the fastidious independence and morbid scruples of Dr. Newman. He was welcomed and rapidly advanced, and, on the death of Cardinal Wiseman, Dr. Manning was promoted to the Archbishopric of Westminster. Up to that time some symptoms of division had shown themselves among the Roman Catholics in England. Dr. Newman, a man of genius, had drawn round himself a small but able party. A periodical had been started by some of them, and that periodical had ventured on Liberal sentiments which had annoyed and startled Rome. The Papal Encyclical was launched as a thunderbolt against these rebels. They were to be taught on the highest authority that the darkest idolatries of the middle ages and the most extravagant claims of Papal ambition were held as firmly and must be obeyed as implicitly under Pius IX. as under a Leo or Borgia. Therefore the periodical was given up, and the men of genius were put down. When Dr. Manning mounted his throne, he ruled over a submissive though sullen Church. Thenceforth it was certain that none would speak his disgust, though many felt it. Dr. Cullen and Dr. Manning had thus become the two absolute chiefs of a docile and united confederacy. It was impossible to find better leaders for the work which had to be done. *Dr. Manning. The two Romish chiefs.*

England lay slumbering, careless, unsuspecting, when the Roman leopard, having crept forward from its ambush till it gained a vantage-ground, was just preparing its final spring on a drowsy and stupefied foe.

The advance of Rome.

The time for a forward movement had come; parties in the House of Commons, though not exactly balanced, were struggling for place. The reign of Lord Palmerston was evidently drawing to a close. Age and infirmities had at length overtaken that vigorous head and the hand of consummate skill. The shelter of his tact and long experience was about to pass away from his party. Already Mr. Gladstone had become restive. In the absence of his chief he was frequently throwing up his heels, and kicking over the traces, and his escapades, while they marked his convictions, proved his rashness. His wayward speculations, his bursts of uncontrollable temper, formed a singular contrast to the tact and reserve of the wary leader. Already he crept to the side of Mr. Bright, asked his advice, and received his counsels. The thoughts of the two men became more and more alike. The passions of the demagogue began to prevail over the habits of the statesman. Impatient, impressionable, impulsive, Mr. Gladstone was deferring daily more and more to extreme views and Republican projects. He began to cater for a low popularity. The friend of Sir Robert Peel, of Sir James Graham, and Sydney Herbert, sought the praises of Potter, Bradlaugh, and Beales.* The associate of the benevolent plans of Archbishop Howley, and Bishop Blomfield, received and returned the praises of Messrs. Miall and Mason Jones. There never had been in public life, since the days when the genius of the Girondins lapsed into the passions of the Jacobins, an example of so sudden and so complete a fall. It was evident to all spectators into what courses Mr. Gladstone was about to precipitate his followers and through what miry ways he would lead them.

Change in the Liberal leaders.

* Another deplorable specimen of this temper appears in Mr. Gladstone's reception of the man Finlen and the rabble rout whom he presented as the working class. Mr. Gladstone's recognition of coarse Sabbath desecration deserves a severer censure.

CHAPTER V.

BOLD ADVANCE OF THE ROMISH HIERARCHY IN 1865, 1866, AND 1867.

THE chiefs of the Romish party saw the opportunity which this change of circumstances and of leaders afforded them, and at once resolved to bring their influence to bear on the weakened Government. The pressure came first from Ireland; Cardinal Cullen made the first move. His proposal turned on education, a subject on which the Romish hierarchy feel justly anxious. For curiosity and intelligence, if they once spread among a people, are sentiments highly dangerous and carefully to be repressed. They are unfavourable to the influence of priests, to their drowsy and deadly reign. Rome is, therefore, careful to take precautions against them. Other despotic Governments, with a blundering fatuity, try to repress intelligence by discouraging schools. The Church of Rome never falls into such a blunder.* She prescribes schools, she sets up schools, she makes Government endow schools; only she takes care to get the schools into her own hands, and, having put in her own creatures as masters, she works them for her ends. She is not such a simpleton as to leave out the people and drive them to secular schools of their own; she attracts or threatens the children into her schools, and then locks them in. Thus she makes them, in childhood, her own. Intellect she subdues, curiosity she represses, but abstract study—arithmetic, even mathematics—she tolerates; catechisms, formularies, observances, legends are her delight. Fictions of silly saints, romances of garbled history, legends of the Church—with these she feeds the young mind; till, drilled and disciplined, crushed and wearied, it resigns itself to its instructors. Thus the children of her schools come forth (like

How Rome deals with schools.

---

* I forget what Romish M.P., Sir G. Bowyer or Mr. Maguire, boasted once of the prevalence of education in Rome. The fact was correct, though the argument was weak. In every Rioni in Rome there is a Government school, and every child must attend it.

42   BOLD ADVANCE OF THE ROMISH HIERARCHY

Romish education.

the students at Maynooth and Clongowes) ignorant of everything in nature or in the past which can open their minds, but mechanical, sharp-witted, armed with arguments against Truth, obedient to the Church of Rome.*

When the Romish hierarchy gave in their adherence to the system of National Education in Ireland, they had two reasons for their decision. First, the demand for education among the Irish people was so strong, that it could not be resisted. The Protestant schools had scattered a thirst for knowledge. If the Romish Bishops did not take what the Whig Government offered them, a system of national schools purely secular and independent of all sects would infallibly have been adopted. By joining the National system, the Romish bishops expected that they would be able to modify and cripple it. Archbishop Murray was on the Commission—a prominent member. No step would be taken without his advice, and, if he could not arrest or frustrate the National scheme, he would certainly secure for the priests a large influence over it. They were right in their calculations. The priests throughout Ireland became patrons of

National Education how dealt with.

the National Schools, and took them into their charge. They put in masters who were the priests' tools. They kept them in, in spite of remonstrances from Dublin. Irregularity of attendance was winked at. The rules of the Board were violated; catechisms were taught at all hours. The children were made to learn as little as it was possible; in many cases they learnt nothing. No school in Rome could have been more regular and more worthless. But the priests had other resources; false returns were made, so that money was had from parliament, and no education was given. Schools were taught by monks, *Les Frères Ignorantins*, worthy of their name. Nuns set up convent schools, in which girls were trained in superstition, and hatred of heretics. By inducing the Board, after Mr. Cardwell's time, to increase the number of nuns who trained mistresses, they secured a succession of teachers as ignorant as could be desired.

Effects of National Education.

Still, in spite of this dexterous policy and its partial success in neutralising the effects of mixed education, the National Schools began to have an influence. Many schools were well taught. Rays of light forced their way through the darkness. A taste for letters,

* A beautiful specimen of this was supplied in St. Mary's Catholic School, Edinburgh. In five years the child could tell his letters, two years more he could put them together, in thirteen years he could just read; and this was held forth by the priests as an education up to the mark of modern demands, yet solid in faith and piety.—Wylie's " Rome and Civil Liberty," p. 135.

a spirit of inquiry began to spread. The Bishops were compelled to publish an edition of the Bible in order to keep their people from reading the Protestant version. There was a demand for the Bible which horrified the priests. A fact also occurred which startled them greatly. It happened during Mr. Cardwell's administration. He had requested* one of the English Inspectors to make a tour in Ireland, and visit the National Schools. The report, which he brought back, was to the friends of education eminently satisfactory. Though far inferior to the schools with which he was familiar in Yorkshire, the Inspector found the Irish National Schools vastly superior to the old hedge schools, or to the schools which Romish priests conducted on the Continent. He made no secret of his impressions, and they transpired and reached the ears of a Romish inspector, who carried the intelligence to Dr. Cullen. Dr. Cullen saw the danger. The National Schools, it was plain, had become a nuisance. Education under secular Commissioners, given by masters well trained and placed in popular schools,—what danger to a Church which could only stand on ignorance! Not a moment was to be lost. Dr. Cullen addressed himself to the task with his usual energy. After various underhand attempts, in 1866 he presented a formal memorial to the Lord-Lieutenant, *signed by all the Roman Catholic Bishops.* That memorial denounced the whole system of National Education, and demanded that the National Schools, as far as they concerned the Roman Catholics, should be placed absolutely in their hands.† Not successful at once in this demand, he modified his plans, and renewed his attack in another direction. *[margin: Interference of Dr. Cullen.]*

In the Session of 1865 the O'Donoghue had been set up in the House of Commons to open a new grievance. With his brief carefully prepared, and the real object kept carefully out of view, he made a plausible case for his Church. He set forth the wrongs of the oppressed hierarchy, and contrasted their mournful destitution with the flourishing state of Trinity College. Nothing was said by him of the legacies which Dr. Cullen and his colleagues had extracted from dying superstition and death-bed fear. Not a whisper of the thousands of pounds which were steadily flowing into their coffers from impoverished families and plundered heirs. These endowments, swelling from *[margin: The Romish Bishops' College.]*

* I state this as mentioned to me by the Inspector himself after his Irish tour.

† See Papers on University and National Education, 5th March, 1866, pages 4, 11, 13, and 16.

year to year, had long overtopped the paltry funds of Trinity College. But of this not a whisper: in rags and tatters, the Romish bishops stood begging at the door of the English Treasury. Give us, they said, a little help for our starving professors and empty college. To be sure, the college was empty, for no lad, who wanted a good education, would go near it; to be sure its professors were ill-paid, for all the threats of the Romish Bishops had failed to drive students from the godless College, where they were taught much, to the Bishops' College, where they were taught nothing. But of this fact not a word—the real design to drill Irish youth in superstition and keep them in ignorance was carefully concealed. The object held forth, which Mr. Gladstone* professed to believe, was to *elevate* and *enlighten* poor, suffering Ireland. So the O'Donoghue made a plausible case, and his appeal for help to the Bishops' College in Ireland was favourably entertained.

The appeal was met, on the part of Lord Palmerston's Government, by Sir George Grey. Neither the Premier nor the Home Secretary had a great liking for their task. It was an ungainly work. They did not enter into it with the relish which Mr. Gladstone felt. They had no fellow-feeling with the Irish Priests and Dr. Cullen. Still the work had to be done, for the general Election was near, and on the course taken by Dr. Cullen and his priests at that election there turned more than 60 votes. Government could not afford to lose these, still less to throw them into the hands of Lord Derby. So Sir George Grey met the O'Donoghue with compliments, fair words, and promises. The promises were vague, and each side could put different interpretations upon them. But the object was gained—expectations were held out, and the Priests voted for the Liberals at the election of 1865.

Whig bargain with Rome.

But there is this characteristic in a bargain between statesmen and the Church of Rome: it is easily made, but it is not easily carried out. A wink and a word make it. The Cardinal catches your meaning from a look, but, when you settle, you have to settle in full. It is the old German story. Mephistopheles is indulgent and caressing when you are selling your soul to him, but he returns, and makes you pay to the last mite. So the unlucky

---

* It is difficult to read such language from Mr. Gladstone, who knows perfectly the character of the education given in good National Schools, and in the Priests' Schools, without feelings of indignation. He must see that he is selling the hopes and the moral life of the Irish people to the priests, for a political consideration.

Government found. For the Home Secretary had not time to enjoy his leisure in August, before Dr. Cullen and Dr. McHale—watchful birds—swooped upon him. Before the election was well over, when the votes sought had hardly been had, the wary ecclesiastics came and demanded the price. Archbishop Leahy* tells us that the plan of the Bishops is, to ask much, and take what they can get. Acting on this principle they spread out large demands, and in this case their demands were exorbitant.† They asked first of Sir George Grey (for it touched them most) a modification of the system of National Education in Ireland. That was the great nuisance; and they told Sir George Grey that it must be put down. They said that the National Schools must pass from secular hands into their own; and, above all, the Model School in Dublin must be suppressed. They did not pretend that it was proselytizing, they did not accuse it of being irreligious. But it was pouring good teachers into Irish schools, therefore it was a nuisance. Their words deserve to be quoted: "Next come the Model Schools, of which the Commissioners of Education are the patrons, and *over which the Catholic Bishops and clergy have no manner of control*, as to teachers, books, or any thing else, and to which, *as being far the most objectionable part of the system*, Catholics do give, and will give, the most determined opposition. But one thing can be done with the schools—to do away with them altogether. Nothing *else will satisfy the Catholic Bishops*, clergy, and people." In effect,‡ their demand was, Give us money and leave the schools to us, to make them as worthless as we can. This demand (*which*

<small>Terms of Rome.</small>

---

* See further correspondence with Lord Mayo.

† See Papers on University and National Education, 5th March, 1866, pp. 4, 9, 10, 11, 13.

‡ This demand is put in the plainest language by Dr. M'Hale, at Castlebar, August 8, 1868. He says,—and it shows how perfectly the truculent Celt and the polished Dr. Manning agree in their demands for Supremacy: Dr. M'Hale, in referring to the Irish landlords and the English Government, "We come here to tell these gentlemen to content themselves with the exercise of their own power, and we are resolved that they must not interfere with us in the exercise of our duties, nor to transgress its limits.........What are these interfering gentry doing to this very hour? Have we the *freedom of education* that belongs to us? It was not said to emperors, or kings, or queens, that they should teach, *an office that exclusively belongs to the Catholic hierarchy.* Yet these presumptuous people have usurped this office, for they have advocated and supported anti-Catholic and anti-National education. Consequently they have attempted the ruin of the faith and morality of the flocks committed to our charge"!! Freedom of education then means, power to the Church of Rome to keep the people in savage ignorance.

Mr. Gladstone is now preparing to grant) was a little too strong for the Whig Government—they refused. But they had promised some help to the College, and something must be done.

After a correspondence, which lasted from August 1865 to January 1866, after a long and fierce struggle, the Cabinet came at last to terms. They * "will advise her Majesty to grant a charter of incorporation to the College founded in Dublin by the Roman Catholic Archbishops for the higher education of youth," and are ready "to grant a sum for the purpose of bourses." Such was the bargain, and Mr. Gladstone, then Chancellor of Exchequer, after engaging to the House of Commons not to carry it out without giving the members an opportunity to discuss it, managed to evade his promise, and so this very discreditable transaction was smuggled through.

Concessions of the Palmerston Government.

Happily legal obstacles intervened and stopped it. The demand of the Bishops was reopened on the Conservative Government, but Lord Mayo took the same ground as Sir George Grey, and insisted still more distinctly on an *effective lay control* over the Senate, a control which Mr. Whittle, Dr. Corrigan, and a large body of independent Roman Catholic laity demanded. This Dr. Cullen and the bishops would not endure, and the negotiation failed. It remains an instructive record of the real aims of Dr. Cullen and the Romish bishops. They want the National-schools and colleges of Ireland in their hands, that they may make the future generations of Ireland as bigoted, as ignorant, and as hostile to England as themselves.

Object of the Romish Bishops.

The nature of this system has been clearly exhibited in the late inquiry into the Italian Colleges by the Italian Government.† It appeared from the inquiry by the Italian Government, that where the Romish bishops have had the entire control over Seminaries (as they seek to have in Ireland)—when they nominate the professors, fix the studies, and settle the rules—so detestable is the education, that even the worthless Despotisms of Modena and Tuscany could not endure it, and the present Italian Government has had no choice but to withdraw the Seminaries entirely from the control of the Romish bishops. Yet to this odious system Messrs. Bright and Gladstone are now preparing to grant millions of the public money, so that Ireland may become worse than the Romagna, and be handed over to a helpless and hopeless degradation.

Bad system, condemned in Italy, approved by Messrs. Bright and Gladstone.

* See papers as above.
† Statistica del Regno d'Italia. Fierenze, Nov. 10, 1865.

CHAPTER VI.

THE SECRET COMPACT AGAINST PROTESTANTISM BETWEEN THE HEADS OF THE ROMISH CHURCH AND MR. GLADSTONE.

WHILE these important schemes, affecting education, occupied the attention of Dr. Cullen and the Irish bishops, Dr. Manning was following his own department of higher and more important labour. His views were as farsighted as Cardinal Cullen's, and soared to a bolder flight. He deals with sovereignty, he must seize the Queen's sceptre. He has told us what he thinks of the Supremacy of the Sovereign,* how abnormal it is and how obsolete. He will have no Sovereignty in England but that of his Papal master. Any other claim, whether made by Parliament or by the English Crown, is heresy and usurpation.† It is kind in him, considering our position as a nation, to come to our help. For nothing, he says, can be sadder than our condition. We are on an inclined plane, which leads us into the gulf of infidelity and revolution. We have sown in our bosom "the principles of heresy and anarchy," and through adherence to the detestable falsehood of the supremacy of our Queen, which is the essence of heresy, (in fact, the "Reformation in Concreto'‡') our Government, "which has headed the unbelief and the sedition of Europe,' and directs the full power of England against the Catholic Church, and above all against the Holy See," is "essentially a denial of the Divine institution of the Church, and represents a population, not only in schism and in heresy, but traditionally hostile to the spiritual authority of the Church and the Pontiffs."§ From this tainted

Assails the Queen.

Royal Supremacy.

---

* Essays on Religion by Dr. Manning. Pp. 18—20.
† Essays on Religion by Dr. Manning. Pp. 410—412, 459.
‡ Essays on Religion by Dr. Manning. Pp. 18, 19.
§ Sermons by Dr. Manning, 1863. Pp. 63—65.

blood, he says, our morbid humours must be drained. So he sets to work with all his heart to recast our Constitution, change the structure of our laws, and upset the authority of our Queen.

A long train. With this view he laid a long train. He began far back, at the Emancipation Act of 1829. It was a bold measure to undo what had given the Roman Catholics their political rights, but Dr. Manning is a bold man. He chose for this great stroke a good occasion and a qualified agent. His agent was Mr. Monsell, M.P. for Limerick County. No one could have been better selected. A Privy Councillor, once in the confidence of the Whigs, he had handled an important office, and was honourably distinguished from the vulgar Members of the Papal Band. He was not a native born of Rome, but a pervert from the Church of England. He understood, therefore, the sentiments of English gentlemen, and was a practised, and, when occasion served, could be a plausible speaker. The rancour of his dislike of the Church, which he had deserted, was covered over by a varnish of fair appearance and seeming candour. Though he could say with truth—

Mr. Monsell.

" My voice is much for open war, my peers,
As not behind in hate,"

and his hatred was, like that of most perverts, strong and deep. Thus he was well fitted to represent Dr. Manning, whose writings show a special hatred of our Crown and Church. And in Dr. Manning's case it added a zest to the pleasures of gratified ambition, that he, who had been held by the English Crown unworthy of an Anglican Bishopric, should have risen by his own exertion to the highest pinnacle of the Roman Church; seated there, should confront his Queen—hurl against her his defiance—seize her sceptre, tear from it its chief jewel, and hand it to the Pope; and then,* denouncing her as a heretic, and proving her unworthy to reign, should set on foot in Parliament his deep and vigorous machinations.

Mr. Monsell's Bill. Mr. Monsell was not a Roman Catholic in 1829, and was therefore not bound by the oath which the Roman Catholic bishops and laity had then contracted. So, before the election of 1865, Mr. Monsell was set up to demand that the Roman Catholic oath of 1829 should be repealed. He did his work well, and Mr. Gladstone, always on the side of Rome, hastened to help him. With such support, and his object so well dis-

* Essays, pp. 457—9, 461.

guised, Mr. Monsell passed his Bill through the House of Commons, though it failed in the House of Lords. But the Lords, though upright, are not strenuous; they are not persistent, and are easily deceived. They are apt to give to great questions a languid and interrupted ear; to borrow, without much inquiry, opinions that float in general society. They heard much of the scandal of oaths; they fancied it was possible to satisfy the Roman Prelates; and so, weary of debate, they let the Government have its way, and the Government, in February, 1866, under Mr. Gladstone's directions, brought in a bill to sweep away oaths.

The history of the Oaths Bill, thus introduced by Sir George Grey as the organ of Lord Russell's Government, is given us by two authorities which cannot be disputed. Mr. Dillon, an instrument of Cardinal Cullen, and, like The O'Donoghue, a member of the Popish National Association, says, in a letter published in the Irish newspaper, that a bargain was struck between Mr. Gladstone and the Papal Band. They, numbering 60 votes, were to vote for the Reform Bill on certain conditions. But let me quote Mr. Dillon's words :— {Mr. Gladstone's Oaths Bill.}

"That course is to give an unconditional support to the Extension of the Franchise Bill. I say unconditional in this sense, that we have not gone to Mr. Gladstone, and demanded formal pledges from him in respect of Irish measures as the price of our votes; but not in the sense *that we are entirely in the dark as to what the Government are likely to do.*"

"The relations of the National Association towards the Government may be thus shortly stated :—The Association has put forward four claims—the reform of the land laws, *the removal of obnoxious oaths*, freedom and equality in education, and the disendowment of the Established Church. The Government concede the first two in full at once, give an instalment of the third, and as to the fourth, *ask us to wait a little, as its hands are full*, bidding us in the meantime 'God speed.'"

In consequence of this bargain the Oaths Bill, the first instalment, was introduced and pressed eagerly through the House of Commons before the Franchise Bill was presented to Parliament. {The bargain of Mr. Gladstone with Dr. Cullen.}

Its passage there, however hurried, brought out some striking facts. Though the country was taken by surprise, and had little time for action, petitions signed by 33,000 Englishmen were presented against the Bill. But the voice of the English people has no effect where Mr. Gladstone has made a bargain with Dr. Manning.

The terms of Mr. Gladstone's Bill involved an entire surrender of the great constitutional principles which Dr. Manning desired to root out. Mr. Disraeli, in Committee, proposed two Amendments—the one recognised the Succession to the Crown as fixed by the Act of Settlement; the other declared the Queen's Supremacy.

Both were opposed fiercely by Messrs. Bright and Gladstone; their compact with the Romish members would have been annulled. To gratify Mr. Bright, the idea of *defending* the Queen against conspirators was struck out. The recognition of the Protestant Succession was, however, carried; the House was not yet prepared for an entire abandonment of its Protestantism. But the declaration of the Queen's Supremacy was lost by a small majority; for this was the hated declaration which Dr. Manning sought especially to expunge, and for this Mr. Gladstone put forth all his energies.

<small>Mr. Gladstone's bargain with Dr. Manning.</small>

Let us now look behind the scenes, and see the real movers. When the Oaths Bill reached the House of Lords, deputies from the Roman Catholics waited on Lord Derby; and the objects of their interview are given by Mr. Wegg Prosser in a letter in the *Tablet*, published April 14, 1866. The great object of the deputies was to carry out Dr. Manning's scheme, and to prevent Lord Derby from inserting in the Oath a Declaration of the Queen's Supremacy. They said it had been difficult to persuade Dr. Manning to endure a reference to the Act of Settlement, but to admit the Queen's supremacy was impossible.

<small>The secret history.</small>

"Mr. Langdale and myself both explained to Mr. Disraeli, who had been present at the interview, and who doubtless informed Lord Derby of what we said, that it was *necessary for us to consult the ecclesiastical authorities* before we could assent to the proposed Amendments.

"Mr. Langdale lost no time in putting the whole matter before the Archbishop (*i. e.* Dr. Manning); but his Grace thought it more prudent, in a question of such importance, to consult the other (Roman Catholic) bishops before giving an opinion.

"Mr. Prosser then expresses his belief that all the Roman Catholic bishops have been consulted as to the oath, and he adds that

"'No good Catholic could take part in enacting such a measure as the Act of Settlement of the Crown, because *it expressly excludes a Catholic from the succession on the very ground of his religion*, and it follows that *no Catholic can share in enacting an Oath to maintain and support that Act of Settlement;* but it does not follow that a

Catholic may not take such oath *when already enacted* by those over whom he has no control.'

"The whole of this he 'submits most respectfully to the judgment of *his ecclesiastical rulers,* to which he is sure *the Catholic laity will bow with strict deference and obedience.*'"

The Roman Catholic *Weekly Register* completes the statement :—

"The Tory Amendment with reference to *the Queen's Supremacy* cannot be accepted, because, if it be the *innocent thing* its parents represent it to be, it is *a platitude which simply means to affront the Catholic subjects of the Crown, and we are not disposed to pocket a gratuitous insult* in order to humour the prejudices of Lord Derby's anti-Catholic supporters. If Lord Derby should invite the House of Lords to disfigure the Oaths Bill by the re-introduction of the Amendment which was rejected by the House of Commons, and should carry his point, *the Bill must be abandoned* as inconsistent in its deformed state with the policy of the Ministerial measure."

Unfortunately, with that fatal disposition to escape conflicts which is the type of the Conservative party, Lord Derby gave way, and this dangerous measure was passed. Mr. Gladstone boasts of the success in the following words at Liverpool :— *Lord Derby surrender.*

"By that measure which is called the Oaths Bill, which we have sent to the House of Lords under circumstances fairer than any other after a century of controversy, all persons holding positions of political trust in either House of Parliament for civil purposes will be wholly and individually released from the necessity of making *any religious profession.* I cannot but congratulate you on this most signal triumph that we have achieved. (Cheers.) I am bound to say that *I have been surprised myself at the facility with which the Bill has progressed in Parliament*—I frankly say that I was not prepared for it; I think that *the obstacles might have been more serious,* but in Parliament it often happens that measures are considered not only in connection with their own merits, but likewise in connection with the merits, prospects, and chances of *other measures impending*—(cheers and laughter)—and it happened that a great subject is coming on in which an important party means to rally all its strength, and exhaust all its powers of opposition; it universally avoids, if it can, committing itself disadvantageously on other measures which may happen to precede it. (Cheers.)"

The struggle, he informed his hearers, was to be on the Electoral Franchise Bill, a Bill, he says, "which did great good before it was born, inasmuch as it formed the passport to the second reading of the Oaths Bill."

From these three witnesses, Messrs. Dillon, Wegg Prosser, and Gladstone, we collect the complete history of this transaction.

1st. From Mr. Dillon we learn that a secret bargain was made with Mr. Gladstone that the Popish members would vote for his Franchise Bill on condition that he assisted their Roman Catholic claims. This part of the transaction Mr. Gladstone in his speech at Liverpool carefully concealed.

Mr. Gladstone's betrayal.

2nd. But he avows that in the absorbing struggle, which was imminent on the Reform Bill, he, according to his bargain, brought on the Oaths Bill, pushed it through with hot haste, as he knew well that the Conservative party, reserving their strength for the Reform battle, would let it slip through.

Either then Mr. Gladstone was an accomplice of Dr. Manning in this matter, or he was made his tool. In either case, let us learn the lesson which the facts teach us. Dr. Manning saw the coming struggle ; he and Dr. Cullen struck in to profit by it. Dr. Cullen gained from Mr. Gladstone an assurance that he would promote the schemes of the Irish National Association. Dr. Manning obtained his promise that he would prepare and press forward a Bill which, beginning with a change in Parliamentary Oaths, was meant to end (as we shall show) in overthrowing the Protestant succession and undermining our Protestant throne.

This is the betrayal of our Protestant principles which Mr. Gladstone has made, and it is the fruit of his secret bargain with the heads* of the Romish Church.

* There is a perfect unity in the Romish plans for obtaining power.

In August, 1851, a monster gathering took place in Dublin, presided over by Dr. Cullen; a Catholic Defence Society was formed, and their objects stated in Resolutions. Every law is to be repealed which hinders what they call "the perfect freedom of the Church" of Rome. 1. Ecclesiastical Titles Act to be repealed. 2. Laws against the Jesuits repealed. 3. All the exceptions in the Emancipation Act, which are five, repealed.

You may think this enough. Far from it. "Such are a few of the objects to which the Catholic Defence Society must direct its attention"!! Its final object is " the perfect independence of the Church, the free exercise and development of its powers "—in other words, its Supremacy, according to the demands of the Pope.—See Wylie, pp. 118, 119.

CHAPTER VII.

THE COMBINED EFFORTS OF DR. MANNING AND MR. GLADSTONE AGAINST OUR PROTESTANT SOVEREIGN.

HAVING obtained this important step through the compact made with Mr. Gladstone, Cardinal Cullen and Dr. Manning combined their efforts to advance their schemes. The Sovereign now stood unguarded. It would be easy to strip her of her faith, or, if she clung obstinately to this, in due time circumstances might arise which would settle the question according to these unalterable principles which Dr. Manning had explained to the public in his luminous work.

Without the loss of a moment, now that Mr. Gladstone had surrendered himself into the hands of the Romish leaders, the order was given to advance and assail the citadel. The first object was to deprive the Queen of her Protestant counsellors, and to surround her with advisers, who should be the accomplices of Rome. The Bill of Rights, and the Act of 1829, had reserved five offices from which Roman Catholics were excluded—that of the Regent; the Commissioner who represents the Sovereign in Scotland; the Lord-Lieutenant, who represents her in Ireland; and her two Lords Chancellor.* Dr. Manning directed his first blow at the outwork, and the tactics were worthy of a veteran campaigner. [Attack on the throne.]

Sir Colman O'Loghlen was selected for this duty, and the selection, as we shall see, was judicious; for Sir Colman has an intrepid assurance which nothing can daunt, and a tenacity which holds to its grasp with the gripe of death.

He first approached the Declaration which the Lord-Lieutenant of Ireland makes, as the test of his Protestantism. The Declaration was, that he does not believe in transubstantiation, and does not worship the mass. How galling such a statement to the ears of a sensitive Privy Councillor! How painful to the fine emotions of Mr. Monsell and Dr. Cullen!

* Dr. Cullen had stated in 1851, that one of *the primary* objects on which the Catholic Defence Society insisted, was the removal of the "Coronation Oath and the Act of Settlement, which limit the possession of the Crown to Protestants."

But if the mischief lay in the words used, the remedy was obvious; let the Lord-Lieutenant declare himself a Protestant, and the offence would cease. But that change would not have advanced the designs of the Church of Rome. The Declaration was to be dropped, *and no test to take its place;* then the next step would open the office to a Romanist. But this adroit scheme must be approached with infinite caution. So, as soon as Sir Colman has prepared his mine, the Romish members, with one voice, exclaim that they do not mean to interfere with the *faith* of the Lord-Lieutenant. Far from it. Drilled by their wily chief they speak with consenting voice thus :—

Tactics of the Romish M.P.'s.

On the 20th March, 1866, Sir C. O'Loghlen, on presenting his Bill, said :—

"He would not, by the Bill he then asked leave to introduce, make any change whatever in the law which excluded Roman Catholics from certain offices; but he would merely put an end to the necessity at present imposed on Protestants, under certain circumstances, to make the declaration. *The declaration was a relic of barbarism which ought to be immediately erased from the statute-book.*"

Mr. Cogan, on the 8th May :—

"The Bill contained a proviso that *nothing contained in it should be construed as giving the Roman Catholics a right to fill the office either of Lord-Lieutenant or Lord Chancellor of Ireland.* The simple object of the measure was to remove a declaration which was at *once offensive and useless,* and he hoped that, in the interests of peace, conciliation, and Christian charity, it would receive the sanction of the House."

Sir George Bowyer, on the 8th of June :—

"The Bill *took away no security from the Protestant Church;* it left the law *untouched which provided that the Lord-Lieutenant and the Lord Chancellor should not be Roman Catholics;* it merely removed what was offensive to the Catholics, and what he thought must be equally offensive to right-minded Protestants who must surely feel uncomfortable in being compelled to make such a declaration."

Sir Patrick O'Brien in the same debate :—

"The Roman Catholics *did not wish to interfere with the existing law;* all they desired to do was to take off the statute-book *phrases* which had for years been creating a bad feeling in Ireland."

It is difficult for Englishmen to realize this profound and unblushing duplicity. The House was reassured by these statements; believed in its simplicity that all that these Members wanted was to get rid of an obnoxious form of declaration, and to substitute one that secured the Protestantism of the Lord-Lieutenant, without offending the feelings of the Romanists; so, with marvellous carelessness, they passed the Bill.

Lord Derby, on July 16, exposed the fallacy, and shewed that no security was substituted for the one that was abandoned, and the Bill was most properly rejected in the House of Lords. *Tactics exposed by Lord Derby.*

This was the story of 1866. But 1867 opened under a brighter sky. The Oaths Bill had now been passed; the acknowledgment of the Sovereign's supremacy had disappeared from the public Oath. Mr. Gladstone, now out of office, was the eager ally of Dr. Manning; he had proved himself the friend of Rome on many important occasions, and his bargain with the Papal party in 1866, which had opened to them so great a progress, convinced them that they had only to ask, and he would be ready to give. So now reassured and confident,* Sir Colman takes his next step. All the protestations, made the year before by the Papal Members—the chorus of brazen voices declaring that they never meant to interfere with the faith of the persons holding any of the five offices reserved—are all trampled under foot. The scheme had served its purpose.

So on February 27, 1867, the gallant knight advances. This time his language changes, and the mask begins to fall.

"He admitted that it (the Offices and Oaths Bill) was a supplement to the last Bill. The object of that Bill was to repeal an obnoxious declaration, *while the present Bill proposed to open several offices to Roman Catholics from which they were excluded by that declaration.* It was therefore a Bill of considerable importance. At the time when Catholic Emancipation was carried there were five offices expressly kept from Roman Catholics. The first was the Regent of the Kingdom; the second, the Lord Chancellorship of England; the third, the Lord Chancellorship of Ireland; the fourth, the Lord Lieutenancy of Ireland; and the fifth, the office of Representative of Her Majesty at the Presbyterian Assembly or Synod at Edinburgh. As to the first of these offices, he did not seek to open it to the Roman Catholics; nor did he propose that a Roman Catholic should be Her Majesty's representative to the Edinburgh Assembly. But the other three offices he thought might be fairly opened to Roman Catholics, and it was with regard to two of these three offices that the Bill professed to deal; for the Bill did not touch the office of Lord Chancellor of England. He was well aware that there were persons whom he might call *Assault on the Queen's Councillors by the Church of Rome.*

---

* Sir Colman O'Loghlen's feelings of regard for England and loyalty to England's Sovereign were fully shown in 1848, when a declaration in favour of Repeal was issued, and among the names of the Secretaries who kindled this firebrand of sedition, we read Colman M. O'Loghlen.—See "Times," April 24, 1848.

'old women of both sexes,' who believed that the Lord Chancellor of England was the keeper of the conscience of the Crown, and that Her Majesty consulted him on every question of faith and conscience. They also thought that the Lord Chancellor had to decide on all questions of doctrine and discipline in the Church of England. *This was all fallacy; but for the present he did not propose to offend these prejudices."*

He then refers to the resistance of Lord Derby, and hints at the further plans by which Dr. Manning seeks to assail the Sovereign :—

"It was true, as was remarked last year by a venerable peer, who assumed the guardianship of Protestant interests in the other House, that the declaration was one which the Sovereign was obliged to make at her coronation; *but this Bill did not interfere with the Sovereign. Whether the obligation to take this declaration ought to be retained by the Sovereign was a matter for consideration;* but this Bill did not apply at all to the Sovereign, but only to certain office-holders under the Crown."

The same triumvirate of Members, who had last year declared that all they sought was to remove an "*offensive* declaration," but not for the world to "change the law which excludes Catholics from certain offices," now insert the following clause in their new Bill : —that " all the Queen's subjects, without reference to their religious belief, shall be eligible to hold the offices of Lord Chancellor and Lord-Lieutenant of Ireland." Thus, by a casuistry which we used to call Jesuitical, but is in fact characteristic of Rome, another great step is gained.

Further step of progress.

A smaller step follows.

Sir Robert Peel and Sir James Graham had foolishly insisted in 1846 that mayors and magistrates should not flaunt the insignia of their office in a Romish chapel. Mr. Gladstone has no such weak scruples. The more of Rome the better; the sooner we are accustomed to its ways and worship the better. So the Bill of the triumvirs provides that every "judicial and corporate officer shall attend his place of worship in his robes of office," and they report to their rejoicing chief that this step, too, is gained.

So now, encouraged by success, perceiving the profound indifference of Parliament, observing both Houses absorbed in party conflicts, the valiant soldiers, under the orders of their chief, fly each to his appointed post, and rush at the vacant walls. Quick, in Dr. Cullen and Dr. Manning's offices, are prepared the weapons which the soldiers carry into Parliament. No blunders in that war office, no confusion there—one commander-in-chief, full magazines, and prompt obedience!

So on February 7, 1867, three Romish Members bring in the Office and Oaths Bill.

On the same day the same triumvirate present a Bill to relieve all who hold office from the Declaration against transubstantiation, against the invocation of saints, and the sacrifice of the mass.

In March, three other Romish Members bring in a Bill to repeal the Ecclesiastical Titles Act. April, as is only right, is yet more productive. In it three Bills blossom. One Bill throws open the Irish churchyards to the priests and their mob; another Bill settles the question of mixed marriages in the interest of Rome; a third, in which the paternal hand of Sir Colman again appears, provides lands for Roman Catholic churches, schools, and glebes, to be held *for ever* by Roman Catholic Bishops!!

The Bill, relieving office-holders from the Declaration, passes the Commons early, and the House of Lords, wearied, assents. The Bill, which grants lands to Roman Catholic Bishops, was in 1867 a little obscure, but it becomes luminous this year, when Mr. Gladstone's plan of handing four millions of our money to Dr. Cullen and the Romish Bishops, looms large on the horizon. But this Bill, effective as it was, had an untimely end. Mr. Newdegate pointed out that it handed over the unfortunate Roman Catholic laity to be the slaves of the Romish Bishops, and this fact, so acceptable to the worthy Prelates, but a little startling to the laity, awoke at length the slumbering House from its dream. The Bill was rejected by 119 to 75.

<small>Weapons from Rome's magazine.</small>

But notwithstanding these rapid steps of progress the Throne of England was still Protestant, and the English people still acknowledged the Supremacy of the Sovereign, and rejected the Supremacy of the Pope. This, as Dr. Manning clearly sees, will never do. It is the source, as he remarks, of all our national evils. So to this grand question all efforts must be turned.

The Roman triumvirs are therefore instructed to slip in a clause into their Office and Oaths Bill. As the conflict would be sure to rage on the first clause, which opens the offices of Lord-Lieutenant and Lord Chancellor in Ireland to Romanists, the 4th clause might escape notice. This clause extends Mr. Gladstone's Oaths Bill to all persons who hold office under the Crown. In this manner it sweeps away the Oath of *Supremacy*, so hateful to Dr. Manning, and it substitutes an oath of allegiance, from which the detested Supremacy of the Queen disappears, and, to make this palatable, a clause is inserted in the oath *recognising the Protestant succession*, as (the new oath once passed and one hateful

<small>Romish art.</small>

doctrine left out) they may effect a further change in another year, and expunge all reference to the Protestant succession to the Crown. This adroit course is carefully followed.

The year 1867 expunges the Sovereign's Supremacy. In 1868, Dr. Manning takes advantage of the conflict of parties, and suggests to the weakened Government that a simple oath of allegiance to the Queen, *her heirs and successors by law established*, would answer all the purpose. Thus the Protestant Succession follows the Royal Supremacy, both drop into the shade* and disappear from public view.

Hereafter, all reference to Supremacy gone, all mention of Acts of Settlement expunged, Sir Colman will find no difficulty, especially when he has a friendly Cabinet, in arguing that the Acts of William III. are obsolete and offensive, and that all that is needful is to promise allegiance to the Queen† and her heirs.

Assault on the Protestantism of the English Crown.

Thus he will relieve the Queen of that odious declaration which he has reserved "as a matter for future consideration," of which he has already relieved her representative in Ireland, as offensive to the Catholics, and a "relic of barbarism which ought to be immediately erased from the statute-book." Then he will reach the consummation, which Dr. Manning holds out to the hopes of the faithful—the reunion of the English Crown "to Christendom by submission to the living authority of the Vicar of Jesus Christ."‡

Then will cease that painful division, which separates the

---

* The answer of Lord Cairns to the question of Lord Shaftesbury (July 16, 1868) is, we need hardly say, able; and, in one point of view, it is conclusive. No one alleges that the Queen's Supremacy or the Protestant succession to the Crown depend on oaths; they depend on Acts of Parliament. But Lord Cairns is far too acute not to see the object which Rome has in view in getting rid of these oaths. If you say *oaths* are of *no* value, why do you insist on them in a court of justice? Whatever value they have there, they have in politics. The reason why Dr. Manning has steadily worked towards this change, and to the denudation of oaths of everything Protestant, is clear. As long as these oaths *declaring* (*not enacting*) the law were in use, no one could argue that the Acts were obsolete. In a short time, Sir Colman, assisted by Mr. Gladstone, will argue that these Acts belong to an obsolete age—have practically fallen into desuetude—and ought to be abolished—and, I venture to whisper in Lord Cairns' ear, they will carry that in the House of Commons. Better have fought the fight in the trenches, than at the gate of the citadel.

† This will carry out the object announced by Dr. Cullen in the monster Meeting of 1851.

‡ Manning's Essays, p. 18.

English Sovereign from the sympathies of millions of her subjects, and which prevents their allegiance to her and her heirs. For as Dr. Manning justly observes,—

"The election of a Prince in a Christian community cannot be put in the category of a purely civil act. If, therefore, an heretical Prince is elected, or *succeeds to the throne,* the Church has a right to say, ' I annul the election, or *I forbid the succession.*' Or again, if *a King of a Christian nation falls into heresy,* he commits an offence against God, . . . and against his people. . . . Therefore it is in the power of the Church, by virtue of the supreme authority with which she is vested by Christ over all Christian men, to *depose such a Prince* in punishment of his spiritual crime, and to preserve his subjects from the danger of being led by his precept and example into heresy or spiritual rebellion."*

Then we shall see those mischievous claims, which our Parliament puts forward to freedom of conscience and of worship disposed of, and the English laws, of which we boast, reduced to their proper dimensions. For, as Dr. Manning† says :—

"The Sovereign Pontiff condemned the pert audacity of those who call upon the Pope to reconcile himself with modern progress. It is for modern progress to reconcile itself with the Pope. The Church cannot yield a jot or a tittle of its Divine laws of unity and truth; the world may renew its ten persecutions, but the Pontiffs will be inflexible to the end. They have counselled, warned, and intreated princes and legislators. If rulers will not hear their voice, *the people will. The pastors know their flocks, and their flocks know them.* The instincts of the masses are Christian, and the tendency of political society is everywhere to the people. The Church is nowhere more vigorous *than where it is in closest sympathy with the people,* as in *Ireland and Poland,* in *America, Australia,* and in *England.*" *Threats of Dr. Manning.*

By this steady application of popular influence under the direction of Dr. Manning, Dr. Cullen, and the Romish priests, what results may not arise ! Already, Dr. Manning tells us, "the state of England shows that the hearts of men are turning backward to a higher and happier law ; they are weary of heresy and schism." They begin to see "that the decrees of Pontiffs, speaking *ex cathedrâ,* or as the Head of the Church, whether by Bull, or Apostolic Letter, or Encyclical, or Brief, undoubtedly emanate from a divine assistance, and are infallible." ‡ The Vicar of Christ

---

* Manning's Essays, pp. 458-9.

† The centenary of St. Peter—a Pastoral Letter to the Clergy, by Henry Edward, Archbishop of Westminster, p. 100. Longman, 1867.

‡ Dr. Manning's "England and Christendom" (Longman, 1867), pp. 79, 105, 7, 8.

"watches over England with the love of a Father," and is "calling his scattered flock to the one fold. Every baptized soul is the sheep of Jesus Christ. . . . He would have them all brought back, he has sent us to call them home."

The home to which Dr. Manning invites us has a vigorous domestic legislation. This appears before us on the highest authority, in the Papal Encyclical of 1864 :—"There is an erroneous opinion, *called by our predecessor, Gregory XVI., an insanity,* that liberty of conscience and worship is each man's personal right. There are also other principal errors of our time, as, the proposition that it is no longer expedient that our religion should be considered as the religion of a State, to the exclusion of all other forms of worship : *that Protestantism is a form of the Christian religion :* that the Church has not the power of dogmatically defining that the Catholic *is the only true religion ; that the Church has no power of employing force ;* that any one immigrating into a Catholic country should be allowed the exercise of his own worship." In that happy land of Erin, where Dr. Cullen will soon prescribe the law, no Protestant worship will be tolerated. As in the brief reign of James II., "of holy memory," it will be put down by force. For Dr. Manning has frankly avowed* that "neither true peace nor true charity recognise tolerance : and that the Church has the right to require of every one to accept her doctrine."

marginal note: The Protestant liberties fall.

Or, as a Romish magazine, the "Rambler," has expressed it, in terse words :—

"Shall I hold out hopes to the Protestant that I will not meddle with his creed, if he will not meddle with mine? No. Catholicism is the most intolerant of creeds. It is intolerance itself because it is truth itself. The impiety of religious liberty is only equalled by its absurdity."

Or to use more recent language taken from Dr. Manning's organ, "The Westminster Gazette," of July 13, 1868 :—

"We cannot, without prevarication, pretend for one moment that there is any other Church in the world than that Church which is spread through all the world—that the one, Holy, Catholic and Apostolic Church, is the only Church, and will be the only Church to the end of the world. She is the only true coin. All the rest are counterfeit, false coin."

marginal note: The Protestant Church disappears.

The end which is so near, the excision of the Protestant

---

* Essays, edited by Dr. Manning, p. 403.

Church and the engrafting of the true Church, is thus described in the "Westminster Gazette," of last June :—

"THE CRISIS.—The time, it seems to us, has now happily arrived in England for the State to withdraw from exclusive association *with an heretical body,* and, in the midst of so many conflicting religious opinions, take up neutral ground. There is no need that this withdrawal should be effected in a spirit hostile to the religious principle of government; on the contrary, the State is bound to promote, as far as lies within its power, and according to its lights, Christian civilization. It is bound now, as heretofore, to act in accordance with the laws of Christian morality, and in obedience to the general precepts of Christian faith. The only change is, that the *State would cease to be identified with one special heresy,* which, however estimable, harmless, and even innocent its individual members may now be, is in itself a direct negation of the will of God. The beneficial importance of such a change cannot be overrated. It is, as it were, as if the State were to be exorcised of the evil which it has been so long possessed of. An enemy has entered into possession, and for more than three hundred years he has held the State in bondage to its evil will, blaspheming in set terms our holy religion, proscribing and persecuting the Catholics of the three kingdoms, and propagating by means of the influence and power of the State its false doctrines among the people. The cessation of this active agency and propagandism of the State in favour of the too long established heresy cannot fail to introduce a fairer and more equitable spirit into our legislation— a more kindly and considerate treatment of the ancient faith. The ban, as it were, under which we have so long lain would be removed. So complete a change as the disestablishment of the Anglican Church involves may well be looked upon as *the inauguration of a new and happier epoch for Catholicism in England.*"

No doubt these brighter prospects, and this advent of a purer age, which shall place England in its true position of subjection to the Church of Rome, require for their accomplishment time and perseverance. But the progress, we agree with Dr. Manning, is steady. There is no halt in the forward march. "The Royal supremacy," due greatly to his pious labours, " has perished. The undying authority of the Holy See is once more an active power in England. The shadow of Peter has fallen again upon it."*

{The Protestant heresy falls.}

Already Dr. Manning confers with Cabinets, enters Downing-street with the step of a master, demands admission to the office of the Home Secretary and the President of the Poor-law, prescribes his august pleasure, and enforces his will. Presidents obey him. Vice-

---

* Essays, p. 20.

Presidents* register his decrees. Already he assumes the Peerage and enters the House of Commons as a Peer. His priests swarm in the lobbies, surround, cajole, and threaten the Members, and by hints of their influence at elections, entrap the unwary, browbeat the timid, and coerce the obstinate.

Their advance in the United States shows the progress which awaits them in England.

"There is nothing even in American progress," says the *Tablet*, "like the progress of the Roman Catholic Church. Its 2,390 churches built in 84 years, its 7 archbishops and 43 suffragans, its 55 religious houses, its 290 colleges and academies, almost all worked by the religious orders. These, great as they are, are only the reddish streaks of the dawn of *a Catholic movement amid the masses*. The Church stands erect amidst the *débris* of the Protestant heresies, which, loosed from the prop of European State Establishment, crash against each other like the pack-ice in a Polar Sea. Heresy is in a state of wholesale disintegration, leading towards a chaos, of which it will be the Church's work in next century to make a cosmos."

The English Parliament defied.

We are apt to talk of the power of Parliament. We fancy that it can pass laws, but we now learn the truth that Parliamentary laws are worthless, unless sanctioned by the Roman Power. For thus their organ speaks of one of our Acts, which Parliament fancied they had passed years ago:—

"What can your new Act want to give it the perfect functions of law? Nothing of solemnity, of force, which the Legislature of the kingdom can give, is wanting; but truly it wants the sanction of religion. The Pope snuffs disdainfully at it. An Italian priest will have none of it. You may print it in your statutes if you please; but before long you will have to repeal and alter it, in order to procure the sanction of a *foreign potentate, without which, in the end, it is simply nothing worth*."

While these signs of the coming supremacy of Rome are gathering round us, it is well to educate the House for the system which is so near. So Sir Colman, of dexterous handicraft, approaches the Queen, and (far more adroit than the blundering Rearden) proceeds to strip her, one by one, of her Royal prerogatives.

* See the remarkable case in the Poor-law of this session when Mr. Villiers and Sir Michael Beach, at opposite sides, vied with each other in deference to Dr. Manning. The proposal was unfair, and contrary to the interests and the independence of the Roman Catholic laity, but it was carried. Sir M. Beach is indignant that a humble Scotch Protestant Society ventures to lay its remonstrance before the House. He has already received the commands of Dr. Manning, and these commands, though most unjust, he implicitly obeys.

This year, undaunted, he heaps Bill on Bill.* One Bill takes from the Queen her prerogative in regard to Irish peers; another disallows her power of granting knighthood; another fixes where she shall reside; another changes the words of her Coronation Oath; another takes away her power over a Public Charity; another disallows her prerogative on Writs of Error. Mr. Goldwin Smith must surely hail this process of denudation as the fulfilment of his sagacious prophecy.† *The English Crown is stripped of its prerogatives,*

But, while all was thus progressive, circumstances arose (a little perhaps from the impatient haste of the Liberal leaders) which revived Protestant suspicion and roused alarm. Mr. Rearden ran indiscreetly beyond his brief, and showed too soon the Papal hand; a storm lowered, and Sir Colman, warned by signs in the sky, withdrew the notice respecting the Royal Oath on which so much depended, which he reserves for more auspicious times. *And of its Protestantism.*

"Sir Colman O'Loghlen,—in Committee on Promissory Oaths Bill,—to move the following Clause :—

"After the passing of this Act, no Sovereign of Great Britain and Ireland shall be required to take, or make, or subscribe, at their Coronation, or on the first day of their first Parliament, whichever shall first happen, or any other time, the declaration, commonly called the Declaration against Transubstantiation and the Invocation of Saints, and the Sacrifice of the Mass, as practised in the Church of Rome, anything in the Bill of Rights or Act of Settlement to the contrary in anywise notwithstanding."

But while we note Sir Colman's labours, let us not forget another measure, well fitted, as Dr. Manning says, "to bend or break that will which nations and kingdoms have found inflexible and invincible!" This remarkable Bill had been presented to the House of Commons, in March, 1867. A Romish triumvirate bore it in, Mr. M'Evoy the chief. The Irish Prelates discountenanced it; they thought it premature. They felt that, with five Bills already on their legs, a sixth might upset the whole. But this Bill was *The Pope mounts the English Throne.*

---

* Attorney-General for Ireland.—*Times*, July 7, 1868.

† Professor Goldwin Smith, March 3, 1868, at the Brighton Town-hall :—
"Looking, however, to the whole state of Europe, no one could shut out the conviction that *the roots of hereditary monarchy* WERE DEAD. (Cheers.) The idea of the right of A PARTICULAR FAMILY *or nation to reign*, and the poetical but irrational primitive feeling in its favour, were gone, and *could not be revived*. The old idea of monarchy had passed away, and the feeling of affection towards Her Majesty was a *purely personal* one. It was plain that in this country monarchy, apart from its social objects, rested on a very weak foundation."

Dr. Manning's, and Dr. Manning must be obeyed. He will teach even Cardinals that his will prevails, and he justly felt that for his objects that brief Bill was essential, for it professed in eleven short lines to do what, since the days of the Norman Conquest, no Pope had dared to propose, and no English Sovereign had endured. It proposed to declare that *henceforth the Pope should have co-ordinate power in England with the Sovereign*, should parcel out dioceses, assign them to his Bishops, grant offices of authority, and confer titles of honour. This prerogative, hitherto confined to our Sovereign by our narrow policy, was henceforth in England to be shared with the Pope.

Mr. Gladstone assists the Pope.

This vigorous project, devised by a far-seeing craft, found in Mr. Gladstone a dutiful supporter. He questioned the prudence of the movement at that moment. He was not sure of its success. The caution which had been shown by the Roman Catholic Bishops "does them the highest honour,"* but his support is ready; "as far as this side of the House is concerned, the Hon. Member will find little difficulty in the prosecution of his enterprise to a successful conclusion." If only Government will support him, "by all means let us go forward with the Bill."

And so this degradation of the British Crown flew forth on the wings of Mr. Gladstone's special favour with the breathings of Mr. Bright's deep sympathy.

Parliament demurs.

But difficulties arose; obstacles intervened; the House did not lend itself with proper docility to Mr. Gladstone's impressions; there arose in the Liberal party a lingering sentiment of regard for English independence. A Committee was appointed; evidence was taken; witnesses, rather indiscreet, were examined; a Report of a Protestant character† was only lost by the casting vote of the Romish Chairman; and the bearing of that valuable measure, which has been so well illustrated by the evidence of Dr. Manning, Bishop Moriarty, and Mr. Hope Scott, began dimly to be seen.

* Debates, March 21, 1867.
† The able Report of Mr. Walpole has this year been fully confirmed by the evidence and Report of the Committee of the House of Lords. I refer every one to that valuable document. It shows us what an escape we have had, and how ready Mr. Gladstone is to surrender the highest prerogatives of the Sovereign to the demands of Dr. Manning. It shows us also that we can put little trust in the leaders of parties in the House of Commons. They all sacrifice anything in order to tide over a difficulty or to avoid a defeat. Let the electors choose manly, resolute members, and hold them to their duty as English Protestants.

England, it appeared, was not yet reduced to the proper standard of submission* to Rome. Though drilled by subtle prelates, and mystified by Mr. Gladstone, it still retained its old-fashioned respect for national independence. There was enough of blundering Protestantism to prevent it going quietly down into the valley of humiliation, and Parliament held fast with a stupid perversity to the rights and prerogatives of its Queen.

* It is well to put in a few words the character of the Government that is to rule us:—1st. The oath which every priest and bishop takes is, "I will attack and persecute heretics" (*Hæreticos et schismaticos . . persequar et impugnabo*). Think of every Protestant clergyman swearing that he would persecute all Dissenters! Nor is this unmeaning: the preaching and the practice correspond. That every man out of the true Church will perish is the belief of all the lower class of Papists, and the effects of such a detestable belief were shown last month in Belgium, where the Belgian colliers crucified their Protestant fellow-workmen, nailing them on a cross till they agreed to worship the Virgin, and *two died from the tortures*. This bigotry affects even the higher class in English atmosphere. At the time of the Papal aggression, Mr. Ambrose Phillips writes to Lord Shrewsbury, "Pray our Holy Father to bestow again and again his apostolic blessing on his children here, who are ready to *combat for his sacred rights*." "We are the children of the crusaders: we will not falter before the sons of Cranmer and John Knox." On the 12th November, 1850, at a public meeting of the Roman Catholics of Manchester, Mr. Henry Turley proposed and carried this Resolution:—"That the Protestant heresy of this country, as a religion, is dangerous to the peace and morals of society." So, when the word of command is given, the Roman Catholics of England and Ireland will rise to carry out their Bishops' oath!! and Mr. Ambrose Phillips and Lord Denbigh show us that they won't want officers.

2nd. If any one asks (as some ignorantly have done) what is the Canon Law, the answer is clear. It is the voice of God to the Papist. It is not a dead letter; but to the priest who administers it, it appertains to say to every Romanist, "to what school a man is to send his child; with whom his son or daughter is to contract marriage; with whom he is to buy and sell; what opinions he is to hold on all political and social questions; *what party he is to support by his vote;* when he may obey the law peaceably, and *when he must meet it with riot and insurrection;* when he may account the Sovereign of the country in which he resides legitimate, and when he must hold his title invalid."—Wylie on Rome and Civil Liberty, pp. 70, 72.

Those who laugh at Rome and the Canon Law had better consult Napoleon the Third. He will tell them that all the blunders of his reign—his two expeditions to Rome; his struggle with the press; his choice of a Jesuit as his Minister of Interior—are all owing to his fear of the enormous power which the Romish priests exert over the French peasantry, which compels him (against his judgment and the interests of his dynasty) to bend and bow to the Roman Catholic hierarchy. (See the remarkable statement of Baron Bunsen on the causes which drove Napoleon to close the Italian war and make peace with Austria—he feared the Pope's excommunication!)

CHAPTER VIII.

THE COMBINED ATTACK OF CARDINAL CULLEN, DR. MANNING, AND MR. GLADSTONE ON THE PROTESTANT CHURCH.

To those who have followed thus far the order of the Roman campaign, it will seem natural that the attack on the Church in Ireland should form the work of the year 1868. That object had been kept steadily in view by Dr. Cullen and Dr. Manning, and to them it was of paramount importance. In this scheme they found, indeed, but little support from their Irish countrymen, and, till they brought pressure to bear, and forced on a spasmodic agitation this year, they had no support from the Irish laity of any class, little even from the priests. The truth is, that in a country so destitute of gentry as Ireland, the farmers and peasants like to see resident gentlemen, and care little whether they wear black coats or blue coats, whether they live in parsonages or in halls. In fact, they prefer the parson, as he is more humble than the squire, more accessible, and, in all their little troubles, more ready to hear and assist them. There were at times combinations against the landlords in Ireland—some were shot at, their stewards were often murdered—but no man for the last thirty years has lifted his hand against the Protestant parson, nor did any one, even the most rabid, venture to lift up his voice against him. So conscious were the priests and agitators of this popular feeling, that they were careful to detach themselves from any movement against the Irish clergy. They left this work to Dr. Cullen and the Bishops. In the last gathering of the Catholic Association, started a few years ago, the members were loud against the Union, and against the tyranny of England; but it was only Dr. Cullen who struck a note against the Irish Church. When the Romish Dean of Limerick and his priests met last winter, they said:

The English Government hated by the Priests.

"We demand the liberation of our country from the domination of the people of England. We claim the land of our forefathers for the benefit of the people whose birthright it is, who have earned by the sweat of their brows the right to live upon, possess, and enjoy it. Our *quarrel is with the Government* who have robbed and murdered our people, and with those who sustain it in its tyranny and usurpation."

In a former year the tenantry of Meath had met under their Romish Bishop, to express their opinion of the state of Ireland; here are their sentiments :—

"The one, the great, the sole question for Ireland is the land question. Other agitations, *such as that against the Established Church*, are got up for party purposes—would infuse an element of bigotry into the already sufficiently disturbed relations between landlord and tenant—would effect the ruin of thousands of tenants, and precipitate that social catastrophe which we are anxious to avert."

Again, the Roman Catholic Bishop Butler, of Limerick, says, "I know there are those in Ireland, and not a few, who regard our subjection to England as a national blessing. . . . I believe, however, that this is not the conviction of the Irish people. I am convinced that the masses of our race, whether at home or abroad, believe and feel directly the reverse. I believe that it is not the feeling of the Irish Bishops or of the Irish priesthood. I know it is not the feeling of either priests or people in Limerick; and I am beyond all doubt sure *that it never was, and it never shall be, the feeling* of your most faithful servant, George Butler."

We have the same sentiments in the *Tablet*. Take a passage, written at the time that the *Tablet* was conducted by Mr. Lucas, the brother-in-law of Mr. John Bright. The writer says :—

"We are perfectly convinced, and on evidence than which demonstration could scarcely be more conclusive, that if the Legislature were to confiscate to-morrow every acre of land, and every shilling of tithe and rent-charge belonging to the Protestant Church Establishment in Ireland, and were to deprive the Protestant bishops and the clergy of every legal privilege which they now possess by virtue of their belonging to the State Church, *they would not have abated the Irish grievance, or cured the Irish disease.*"

The reason of this popular predilection for a Protestant Church throughout the Roman Catholic provinces is plain; the Irish people are attached to the Protestant clergy for two reasons. First, they find in them courteous and charitable neighbours.*

<small>The Protestant Church loved by the Irish peasants.</small>

* Mr. Senior's friend confirms this view; he says that the Roman Catholic laity regard with horror "the project of separate grants for educational pur-

Secondly, and above all, they form a rampart against the exactions and oppressions of their priests. For under these exactions both farmers and peasants groan, though they dare not speak. If they were to speak, their trade would suffer, their labour would be taken from them, even their lives would be in danger.

The Irish peasant obeys but dreads the priest.

Under such circumstances, it is a great resource to be able to steal under cover of night to the parsonage, and confide to a man, on whom they can rely, their troubles or their treasures. The amount received in deposits from Roman Catholic peasants by the Protestant clergy, may be judged of from this fact : in one town in the east of Ireland (I have, for obvious reasons, withheld the name of the clergyman and the place) a clergyman found that he had received in one year 5,000*l.* in small sums from Roman Catholics, who were either going abroad, or who had emigrated and sent money back to their friends in Ireland.

But for this reason, the Romish Bishops hate and dread the Irish Church. They are right ; whenever the Protestant Church is swept away, they will reign supreme. But there is another reason ; they fear the moral power of the Irish Church, and dread its growing influence.

The Irish Church dreaded by the Romish Bishops.

Some letters published in 1851, in the "Dublin Evening Post"* and in the "Tablet," † sounded the alarm on this subject. In 1856, three letters appeared in the "Freeman's Journal," said to be "by an eminent Roman Catholic," from which I quote one sentence :—
" We behold now within this city (Dublin) more than twenty proselytizing establishments, drawing into their vortices about 5,000 Catholics, yearly bringing hundreds to apostasy." In 1855, 1856,

poses. They feel that they cannot control or even check their own clergy, and that the effect of such grants would be the rearing of their children in (as one of them said to me) intolerance, bigotry, and treason. Their earnest wish is that the Liberal Protestants and the Queen's Government would stand between them and these ultramontane tyrants." It is to these tyrants that Messrs. Bright and Gladstone are now seeking to hand over the Roman Catholic laity of Ireland.

* " We learn from unquestionable Catholic authority that the success of the proselytism in almost every part of the country, and we are told in the metropolis, is beyond all that the worst misgiving could have dreamt of."— *Dublin Evening Post*, Nov. 11, 1851.

† " We repeat that it is not Tuam, nor Cashel, nor Armagh, that are the chief seats of successful proselytism, but that very city, Dublin, in which we live." —*Tablet*, November 8, 1851.

and 1860, Dr. Cullen published pastoral letters, of which we append some extracts in a note.*

As long as the Church of Ireland exists this danger is imminent; if the Irish clergy were more active, conversions would spread more widely. It, therefore, became necessary for the safety of the Romish Bishops, that a Church so mischievous should be put down. On this point Drs. Cullen and Manning were thoroughly agreed. But it was long before they could conquer the difficulties which surrounded the question, and the reluctance of their own members to face it. This was shown remarkably in the year 1865. At the *beginning* of that session, Mr. Hennessy, the chosen of Dr. Cullen, opened in Parliament a discussion on the state of Ireland. He and other Romish members spoke of the condition of the country; it was suffering from emigration; it was poor. They begged for money; for, as Mr. Roebuck said, "the Irish members always come to Parliament as beggars." But among all their wrongs, they never alluded to the Irish Church; so that Mr. Roebuck observed with truth, that Ireland, for a wonder, was without a grievance.

The Roman Catholic laity shrink from attack on the Irish Church in Feb. 1865.

But during the autumn of 1864 and the winter of 1865, there had been, as we are now informed, a secret, but significant, negotia-

1865. Mr. Gladstone attacks the Irish Church in March, 1865.

---

* " As in times of danger, *great and extraordinary precautions are necessary,* we have appointed a General Committee, consisting of all the parish priests of the city, the heads of religious orders, and some other members of the clergy, to watch over and check the *progress of proselytism*. Local Committees have also been established to act in concert with the General Committee. ....We exhort most earnestly all the excellent Confraternities, the various admirable associations of gentlemen and ladies of St. Vincent of Paul, all other religious Societies, and all zealous Catholics, to co-operate in this good work, and to unite in defence of their holy religion." (" Dr. Cullen's Pastoral Letter on Proselytism, 1856.") In another letter he exclaims, " Who will give water to my head, and a fountain of tears to my eyes, to weep over the ruin and desolation caused, especially amongst unsuspecting youth, by the infidel and immoral publications which spread like a torrent over the land, and hurry on to perdition *innumerable souls* that have been redeemed by the precious blood of Jesus Christ......Ought we not to have recourse with increased fervour to the powerful intercession of our HEAVENLY MOTHER—the help of Christians, the protectress of the Church, the advocate of the Faithful? Let us all lay our wants before her, let us invoke her in all our trials, let us implore her to protect us from all the evils to which we are exposed in this stormy world, and, above all, to preserve for us that true Catholic faith, without which it is impossible to be saved." (See " Dr. Cullen's Pastoral Letters on the Feast of the Immaculate Conception of B.V.M., 1855 and 1860.")

tion. The Liberation Society, finding that their attack on the Church of England went on heavily, bethought themselves of the help they might gain from the Romish Church. They sent deputies to Ireland; and a Roman Catholic layman now boasts that he was the medium between them and Dr. Cullen. Where the interests of both parties were the same, the compact was easily made.

Compact between Rome and the Liberation Society. The object was to strike down the Church of England; and it was obviously prudent to attack it in its weakest part. So the bargain was struck, and all the more readily that in 1836 O'Connell had shown them the way. The leaders on both sides, being agreed, ordered a forward movement. The Liberation Party contributed the mover, Dr. Cullen supplied the seconder. So quietly was this arranged, that Mr. Hennessy and Mr. Monsell, though much in the confidence of the Romish prelates, knew nothing of it, and never alluded to the Irish Church in the debate of February, 1865. But in March of that year, the arrangements being now complete, Mr. Dillwyn, who represented the Liberation Society, brought forward a motion against the Irish Church, which was seconded by The O'Donoghue, the pupil of Dr. Cullen. That debate was remarkable, or, as Mr. Grant Duff expressed it, *historical*. For it was on this occasion that Mr. Gladstone broke loose from the restraints of the Palmerston Cabinet. He had for some time impatiently borne his secondary position. He was aiming at independent supremacy. He had dealt a stroke for this in his memorable speech on the Suffrage, where he had made a tender for the support of the Radicals. The Irish Church offered him another and a still more important occasion. For before Mr. Gladstone could gain the cordial support of the Voluntaries, he had to wash off the stain of his regard for the Church of England. From that leprosy he must purge himself, and stand clear. This, then, was his opportunity; for Lord Palmerston had resolved to maintain the Church of Ireland, sagaciously as a prudent statesman, firmly as a temperate politician; he had adopted the views of Sir Robert Peel, that "an attack upon the Established Church in Ireland is but a necessary preliminary to an attack on the Established Church in this country;" and of Lord Plunket, who had said, " he considered the Established Church the great bond of union between the two countries: and if ever that unfortunate moment should arrive when they should rashly lay their hands on the property of the Church, to rob it of its rights, that would seal the doom and separate the connexion between the two countries."

Messrs. Dillwyn and O'Donoghue.

Accordingly Sir George Grey was instructed by the Cabinet to resist Mr. Dillwyn's Motion; and it was after this speech that Mr. Gladstone flung himself into the arena and hoisted his green flag of rebellion against the Church. To him it was a stroke peculiarly satisfactory; for at one blow he cut off his connexion with the Church of England, of which he was weary, and threw in his lot with the Voluntaries, to whom he had been long tending; at the same time he assisted the tactics of Cardinal Cullen and Dr. Manning, with whom he had been for some time closely allied.

Mr. Gladstone found, during the same session, another opportunity to advance the schemes of the Romish party, and this, too, was a characteristic occasion. On the 20th June, when The O'Donoghue brought forward a Motion for assistance to a college in Ireland, to be governed by the Romish bishops, Sir George Grey, as the spokesman of Lord Palmerston, had given a vague and chilling promise of assistance. But the reserve, which in his speech betrayed Protestant sympathies, was distasteful to Mr. Gladstone. He watched his opportunity to neutralize and balance it. So, when some Protestant Members denounced the project, and argued that it was a monstrous thing to favour a bigoted college under the charge of Dr. Cullen, and to discourage the Secular colleges which had originated with Sir Robert Peel, and were doing much service, Mr. Gladstone rushed to the rescue. No member of the Brass Band could have struck in with louder vehemence. The facts were all against him. His own position was awkward. He had been a Member of Sir Robert Peel's Cabinet when these very Secular Colleges were established. He had heard, at least he had read,* the speeches of Sir James Graham and Sir Robert Peel. He was aware that these colleges, accepted by all parties, except O'Connell and the Romish bishops, had been established by Sir Robert Peel as a permanent blessing to Ireland.

Mr. Gladstone for Romish university in place of Secular colleges.

But Mr. Gladstone proved equal to the occasion. These colleges, he argued, "were never meant to be permanent, they were set up as a temporary expedient by Sir Robert Peel;" could any man imagine that that great Statesman intended to oppose the inculcation of religion in its most distinct and definite form? "We are acting in the spirit of the policy of 1845."

Thus Mr. Gladstone was able again to render admirable service to Dr. Cullen; and, by handing over the unlucky Irish students to ignorance and Romish superstition, he proved himself the effective

* I rather think he was then out of Parliament.

friend of the Romish hierarchy. Such were his doings in 1865, and from these we pass to the debates of 1866.

1866. Fenian Conpiracy.
In that year there was no longer any talk of tranquillity. Fenianism was rampant, disaffection was general in Ireland. The O'Donoghue dwelt on this in the debate on the Address; for Dr. Cullen had now tacked about, and, as he was moving on a different line, there presented itself before him a splendid opportunity for a blow on a weak Government; he knew that threats are more powerful than prayers, and when priests* can point to four millions disaffected, and ready to rise, they may hope to extort by fear, what they fail to gain by favour. So The O'Donoghue was instructed to make the most of Irish disaffection, to threaten and alarm the Government! Accordingly, in his speech, he dwelt on the signs of danger. He said that the Irish were a highly moral and religious people (that was a compliment to the priests); but that they hated England, and, if they dared, they would rebel. Mr. Blake, the seconder, said, the only way that he could keep his neighbours from rebellion was by assuring them that England was too strong, and that a rising was hopeless.

Mr. Bright favours the Fenians in 1866.
At this stage in the discussion (though on a later day), Mr. Bright interposed. He, too, had long fixed his eyes on Ireland as a useful ally. He had lately visited it. He, like the Liberation Society, had perceived that, for the objects he had in view, much might be made of the Romish Confederacy. His policy, tending to the destruction of English institutions, might draw, as he observed, powerful support from the Romish party. To that party *family connection* had long bound him; but far more common interests, and common hatred of England. Therefore, when, on a memorable Saturday, the suspension of the Habeas Corpus Act was pushed through by the Whig Government, he stood up, the solitary Englishman, to abuse this necessary measure; he reviled England with a hatred as outspoken as Cardinal Cullen, and he gloated over the rebellious antipathies and the general disaffection of Ireland. Justly rebuked by Mr. Roebuck for his scandalous speech, he had received, what he sought, the confidence of the Fenians; and he had been chosen by their supporters to present a petition, which, by its frank declaration of sympathy with rebels, had surprised and startled the House.†

---

* The same argument is used in Prussia. The priests point to nine millions, and demand that nothing be said or done to offend them.

† TREATMENT OF THE FENIAN PRISONERS.—Mr. BRIGHT.—I wish, Sir, to

Still, in all these debates of the spring of 1866, when Irish members were discussing Irish wrongs, and Mr. Bright was raking in the ashes of national antipathy, the Irish Church was never dwelt upon as a grievance. The O'Donoghue alluded to it, but it was a mere allusion. Mr. Maguire abused everything, and therefore abused the Protestant Church ; but, notwithstanding the instructions of Dr. Cullen, the other Irish speakers, even Mr. Bright, passed it by. With Sir Winston Barron the alleged grievance was the refusal to endow the Bishops' College ; with Mr. Rearden it was Irish fisheries ; with others the Land question. Strange to say, this, which is now called the master-grievance, was passed by and forgotten.

But, in the year after, in May, 1867, Sir John Gray was peremptorily ordered to the front by the two Romish leaders, and then the Irish Church came clearly into view. For this there was a special reason. By this time, Lord Palmerston was dead ; the brief Government of Lord Russell had expired ; and the Liberal leader in the Lower House, out of office, and having lost a section of his party, was eagerly looking for some question which would restore him the confidence of the Liberals, and re-unite them under his standard. What was more likely than an Irish question, and a blow directed against the weakest part of the Church of England ? What was more important for the

1867. Assault on the Irish Church ordered, and why.

present a petition, which is signed by twelve or thirteen gentlemen, well known, I believe, to many members of this House, as men of first-class education and position. The Hon. Member proceeded to read the petition, which described Ireland as kept in a state of hopeless subjection in order to maintain the interests of the Irish Church Establishment, a system of land tenure at variance with the feelings and interests of the people and the present distribution of political power ; that the Irish nation, in consequence of the utter hopelessness of a remedy for the evils under which they suffer—

Mr. B. COCHRANE.—I rise to order. I wish, Sir, to know whether the Hon. Gentleman is entitled to make a speech on the Irish question under colour of presenting a petition. (Hear, hear.)

The SPEAKER.—The Hon. Member is perfectly in order. (Hear, hear.) He states that the petition contains such and such allegations. In doing so he is perfectly in order. (Hear, hear.)

Mr. BRIGHT.—The petitioners state that in the apparent hopelessness of a remedy for the evils which press on their country, honourable Irishmen, however mistaken, may feel justified in resorting to force ("Oh, oh!") ; that, in a word, there are legitimate grounds for the chronic discontent of which Fenianism is the expression, and, therefore, some palliation for the errors of Fenians. (" Oh, oh !")—*Times.*

Romish Prelates than to pledge Mr. Gladstone again on the question of the Irish Church? His speech they had had before, but, owing to Lord Palmerston's influence, they had lost his vote. Now the hated Cæsar was dead, and his successor was on the steps of the throne. In him, at least, they were sure to find a friend.

Sir J. Gray's motion, and Mr. Gladstone's speech. So Sir John Gray received instructions from his chiefs; and on the 6th May he made his motion against the Church of Ireland. The motion answered its purpose; it drew out Mr. Gladstone. His speech, in its bitterness, his defiance of his past opinions, and his cynical assertion of his new views, left to Drs. Cullen and Manning nothing that could be desired. The Duke of Argyll has, this session, pointed to that speech as explicit; the Duke is right. Neither Mr. Dillwyn for the Voluntaries, nor The O'Donoghue for the Romanists, could have spoken more distinctly. There was, indeed, one argument in his speech, which no one but Mr. Gladstone could have used, and which Macchiavelli would have envied. He had once maintained, that truth was the mission of a Church, supported by a State; on that ground he had maintained the Church of Ireland, and had refused to endow the College of Maynooth. But he turned now with fierceness upon those who held his opinions; he asked, with bitter scorn, how they could pretend to support a Protestant Church on the ground of truth, when they had been led by himself and others to pay a priesthood, who, as they held, taught falsehood, and who certainly taught the people that no truth was to be found in the Church of England? This superb contempt for the opinions, which he had held and abandoned, was characteristic. There had been nothing like it in former times.

Close of 1867. These incidents and these arguments close our Review of the Parliamentary history of 1867. The curtain is about to rise on a new scene. We shall find indeed the same actors and, in part, the same drama; but the footlights are more brilliant, with a grand display of stage-thunder. And the story, in its licentious extravagance, would satisfy even those foreign spectators, who, looking at us from their position as members of the Church of Rome, detest, and wish to destroy, the Protestant Church in England.

CHAPTER IX.

THE PROTESTANT CHURCH IN IRELAND: ITS PLACE AND MISSION.

WE now approach the point at which the heads of the Roman Confederacy had long been aiming. Through great difficulties, and obstacles intervening both in England and Ireland, they had at last gained the end of their labours, and were near the walls of the Protestant Church. They had placed their mine under its weakest part, and were putting forth their torch to kindle it.

Their army was composed of various sections, whom they had combined in their ranks. And their leaders could not regard, without a flush of satisfaction, the opposite parties whom they had induced to act with them. There were the philosophers, who laughed at the fables of the Church of Rome; there were the Liberal politicians, who insisted on freedom of conscience and liberty of thought. There were the most advanced among the Dissenters, who had for years denounced Rome as the type of every abomination. There was a large section of the Free Church of Scotland, who had for thirty years been the loudest in denouncing the idolatries of Rome. It was impossible that Drs. Cullen and Manning should not look without a smile of satisfaction at the troops enlisted under their banner. To see Mr. Spurgeon, who had thundered against them in his Tabernacle, Mr. Binney, and Mr. Newman Hall, walking under the Papal flag; to find Dr. Candlish and Sir Henry Moncrieff lead up a section of the Free Church into the ranks of the Roman army, and assist the leaders of the Inquisition, was a new pleasure—an evidence of their consummate skill.

State of affairs in 1868.

Respecting the Parliamentary leaders, there was, indeed, no longer difficulty or doubt. Sir Robert Peel was dead; Lord Palmerston was gone; Earl Russell had sunk into a subaltern.

Whereas the leaders now before them had been long known, and were thoroughly trusted. Mr. Gladstone, impulsive, irritable, and fierce against those who crossed his plans, would, now that he had embarked on his crusade of destruction, become only more vindictive. Mr. Bright was even more reliable. His hatred of the Protestant Church, indeed of all our institutions, was as vehement as that of Dr. Cullen. There was no mine the priests could fill with materials to blow up our Constitution, to which he would not gladly offer his help, the Guy Fawkes of modern practice—with a tongue, instead of a torch, more inflammable, and sure not to fail in combustion. Such leaders were prepared for the work at hand.

<small>Uses of the Irish Protestant Church.</small>

And this brings me to the question which, as far as I have noticed, has not been sufficiently explained in late discussions, "What is it that makes the Protestant Church in Ireland a hindrance to the ultimate designs of the Church of Rome? And what makes it (anomalous as it appears to be) so important for England to maintain it?" I shall treat this as a question of policy, without reference to sentimental reasoning. I shall not allude, on the one hand, like Mr. Gladstone, to the piety and labours of the Irish clergy; nor shall I accept Mr. Bright in his new character of a preacher of righteousness. I notice that, when there are imported into our debates parodies of recondite principle, these are employed (as was the case in the French Revolution) by politicians who, having no solid grounds of policy to recommend their projects, appeal to fanciful notions of abstract theory.

One would imagine, on reading the speeches of Messrs. Gladstone and Bright, that English statesmen had, for the first time, discovered the principles of political righteousness; and that all, who went before them, were either so dull that they could not comprehend these, or so unprincipled that they would not apply them. But this suggestion is neither decent nor rational; for, if we rate these two Liberal leaders as high as I have lately read in a bombastic panegyric on Mr. Gladstone, it will hardly be argued that he is as far-seeing as Mr. Pitt, or as calm and sagacious as Sir Robert Peel. Yet the first of these great statesmen made the Church of Ireland, by a national treaty, an integral part of the Church of England: and the latter repeatedly recorded his opinion, that, if the Church in Ireland were destroyed, the Church of England would fall.

<small>William III., his policy in Scotland.</small>

There was a third statesman more illustrious than either, to whom (I beg pardon of Dr. Manning for the remark) England is apt to ascribe her liberties—one whom our late lamented Prince Consort held up to us as a great example, and whom the deliberate judgment of Lord Macaulay has placed on the highest pedestal of reputation. On what ground then did William III., when he set aside Episcopacy, and set up Presbytery in Scotland, maintain a Protestant Church in Ireland, and refuse to endow the Church of Rome? The grounds must have been weighty to move such an understanding; they were grounds of policy, not of passion; for this eminent man has been often charged with Dutch coldness, never with fanaticism.

Let us then observe his treatment of the two Churches in the two countries with which England is closely allied, on a union with which she depends for her peace and strength. He hesitated long, as we learn, what course he ought to take in Scotland, where religious feeling had ran high and produced great disorders. He saw the advantage of one Church and one form of religion for a nation. He knew that religious union was the best basis of civil unity. He felt that a rivalry between two national Churches might cause disputes and divisions. But, after carefully examining the question, he decided in favour of a Presbyterian Church in the northern part of his dominions, and his reasons were these:—

1st. He observed that the Presbyterian Church had the same faith as the Church of England, and the same standard of morals. The Bible was the rule of both, laid on both the same moral restraints, and gave to both the same social impulses.

2nd. He observed that the clergy of the Scotch Church were not celibates—not severed from society into a distinct class with interests apart—but, as husbands and fathers, they had the same interest as other men in the wellbeing of the nation. They did not live by themselves, absorbed in one exclusive passion to aggrandize the Corporation to which they belonged, but they felt a sympathy with social progress, as on this their families depended for livelihood and advancement.

3rd. He found that they were pastors, not priests. The one assume to themselves an authority distinct and special, endowed with supernatural powers;* sitting as gods to hear confessions, and absolve from sin; demanding the secrets of the human heart, and

Political uses of the Presbyterian Church

---

* Most priests, like many of our Anglican Ritualists, value their position as an instrument of power, but some regard it with a sincere conviction, and the idea which these men have of its inherent power is one of the most curious illustrations of the delusions of the human mind. Le Curé d'Ars (and a holier man there

enjoining penance or reparation. By this system enormous power passes into the hands of a few—power over morbid or scrupulous consciences, and, with power, wealth. Of these claims nothing was known in the Presbyterian Church. The Presbyterian ministers pretended to nothing but training for a special calling. They presented themselves as preachers, not priests; preachers of the Divine Word revealed to all; preachers of morality and truth.

4th. William III. saw that whereas priests, by whatever name they are called, in whatever age or country—Augurs, or Brahmins, or Fakeers, or Sacrificers of the Mass—hold their power over the human heart by miracles, oracles, legends, and lies, and the more these are credited, the greater is their power; hence it becomes their interest to keep the people ignorant, in order to make them credulous: the Presbyterian Church, on the contrary, as it appealed for its defence to reason, had from the outset made education a part of its plan, and had opened in every parish a well-taught school. Therefore this great man saw that, whatever defects* the Presbyterian Church might have in the eyes of theologians, it was a matter of indifference to a politician which Church, Episcopal or Presbyterian, prevailed. And if the people beyond the Tweed preferred the simpler forms of Presbytery, it did not become a wary statesman to resist their will.

The Policy of the Church of Rome.

But he saw, with equal clearness, that to set up the Church of Rome in Ireland, to give it influence and authority there, was to plant in the heart of his dominions a hostile confederacy; and to secure, through this, first, the disorganizing of his empire, and then its dismemberment. For he knew the maxims of the Church of Rome, and its polity; that hers was not a theological system, but a Government—a confederacy of the subtlest minds against the fortunes and liberties of mankind; that her plan was to send out agents, called priests, into every nation, and to make the first agents open the door to the next; and to follow these by officers who should rule them, so that the whole force might be united and move together. Thus they would advance, scattering their positions, and occupying fortresses. Into their chapels, they drew men by

never was) deliberately writes, that a priest is far higher than an angel; an angel cannot bring God down from heaven to the altar, a priest can; an angel cannot make God, a priest can; an angel cannot absolve from sin, a priest can. Thus the hallucinations of frenzy become the convictions of faith.

* As I well know the dexterous ability of Mr. Coleridge as a speaker, I point to the weakness of his argument on this point at Exeter, as confirmation of my position. Had there been anything to say, Mr. Coleridge would have said it well.

allurements of sense; and, when drawn there, they appealed to them by motives deep and sure—terrors of the future, reflections on the past, stings of remorse, offers of indulgence, and assurances of safety, to be had by service or bought by money. By these appeals the conscience would be goaded or its uneasiness soothed; while to the Church wealth would flow abundantly, either in streamlets into the priests' hands through rills of daily masses, or by gushes of money and gifts of land, wrenched from expectant heirs by death-bed fears.

In this way, in every nation, priests would multiply, wealth would be gained, position and power would follow, and regiments would march forward under the orders of their Bishops, while the Bishops depended for promotion on the central Government in Rome.* For to Rome every Bishop and priest is bound by oaths of fealty, oaths which oblige them to discard the laws of their nation, and to attend exclusively to the orders of the Pope; and to Rome every priest looks as his Mecca, and, once in three years, every Bishop resorts there to report his acts and receive his orders.

Yet, though Rome was thus made the centre of the system, and the Pope nominally its pivot, the machine was so constructed as to be independent of individuals. A Pope might be, often was, a dotard or a debauchee; but the machine went on untouched by his faults. For it is the cabinet of Rome which governs, and the cabinet never dies; its members drop, but its traditions survive. It lives in the experience of the men who work it, and in the records of its past practice. It draws its intelligence from every nation, and from every tongue and race. It has no restraint to encumber it, for moral laws and Divine rules have no power to bind it. Its maxims are few, and the precepts of the moral law, oaths, and obligations fall, like gossamer, before it. *The Papal System admirable.*

That is right which serves the Church of Rome. That is true which the Church says. That, which is for the Church's interest, is good: crime or vice are virtues, if they help the Church. *Its maxims simple.*

By these simple rules the Roman cabinet acts, and by these it prevails. Kings cross its path, and they fall; emperors confront it, and they perish; cardinals intrigue against it, and they die; premiers defy it, and they pass away. Its movement is that of the simoom—noiseless, but inevitable—all that stand against

---

* This is the reason why the Pope settled his Bishops in England, and struggles so hard for their diocesan functions.

it droop and wither. Its agents are scattered through every land; monks, friars, priests, bishops, legates, cardinals; its councils are fathomless as the sea, and silent as the grave; its action is universal, and sure as the winds.

This was the confederacy by which William III. felt himself confronted, and with which, through all his life, he had to contend. It roused against him the power of France under Louis Quatorze; it raised against him the councils of Spain; it moved against him the blundering cabinet of St. James's; it even inspired the heavy dulness of James II.

Power of Church of Rome in Ireland.

But of all the places, in which its power was greatest and its influence most uncontrolled, was the savage country occupied by the Celtic races of Ireland. There the priests ruled and their supremacy was undisputed. They governed the nation, except only a small section in Dublin and the stalwart colonists of Ulster. To Ireland, therefore, the Roman cabinet looked with confidence as their own; there they raised levies and concerted plans. When the fit time came, the nation rose at their call; in insurgency, as in 1641; in conspiracy, as in 1690; to assist the French, in 1794; to cope with the English arms in 1798. To give to such a confederacy the influence of a State Church would have been, on the part of a Sovereign of England, an act of drivelling folly, of which no able statesman could be capable—certainly not William III.

Reasons for William III.'s policy.

We should have liked to see the stare of indignant wonder with which he would have received such a proposal, had there been in his day a Mr. Gladstone or a Mr. Bright to make it. How, not condescending to argue, and not stooping to explain, he would have ordered such councillors from his presence, as either unworthy from their incapacity to sit in his cabinet, or disloyal because conspiring with his enemies. And if there had been in his days a House of Commons so weak as to suggest that he should strengthen the Church of Rome in Ireland, with what triumphant reasons he would have met and silenced them. He would have shown them that there was no hope of preserving the British Empire, or maintaining the connexion with Ireland, except by cherishing those true-hearted Protestants who alone were loyal to Britain, and by spreading fast and far that Protestant faith which alone could bind in one the dissevered fragments of the British empire.

This was the ground on which that eminent man upheld the Irish Protestant Church, and that ground has been strengthened a hundred-fold by the increased numbers and augmented influence of the Irish Priesthood, by their concentration under one or two unscrupulous heads, and by their combination with the dangerous elements in England which now seek to break up the Empire.

That Mr. Bright, who has presented petitions of Fenian sympathisers,* and has hinted that the time for Repeal may be near, should propose to hand over Ireland, its schools, and its people to the unchecked influence of the Romish conspirators will surprise no one. It is natural that a politician, who dislikes all that is peculiar in our English Institutions, should give his hand to priests who hate our Protestant Church and Throne. But that any statesman, who professes a wish to maintain the integrity of our empire, should lend himself to such designs, is so strange that we ask, whether these acts are consistent with common judgment, or, if the judgment be there, with common loyalty.

But while we speak of the policy of William III. it must be borne in mind that he is not responsible for the misconduct of those who succeeded him. He intended that the Protestant Church in Ireland should be served by qualified pastors, and should aim at National services; he never meant that it should be the refuge of the destitute, and, worse still, the asylum of vice; yet such it too often became in the eighteenth century, through the indifference and the sordid jobbery of the English ministers. They suffered the Irish landlords to rob the Church. They allowed the Irish Parliament to take away a large portion of its tithe. They permitted its churches to fall into decay, and its parsonages to become uninhabitable—then, by uniting livings, and by granting licence for non-residence, they made its ministrations ineffective. So that even in the times just before ours the Irish Church was the scandal of the country, and its dignities were given to men who were too

Abuse of the Church of Ireland.

---

* Mr. Bright, at Limerick, July 14th, 1868, says, he judges from the cheers that his audience think the "only true and lasting remedy for Irish discontent is to be found either in the repeal of the Act of Union or in absolute independence. Well, I blame nobody for holding this opinion. I am one of those who admit, as every sensible man, I think, must admit, that an Act, which the Parliament of the United Kingdom has passed, the Parliament can repeal; and, further, I am willing to admit, what everybody in England admits, with regard to every foreign country, that any nation, believing it to be its interest, has a right both to wish for and to strive for national independence."

On such language from an *English* preacher of political rightcousness comment is needless.

inefficient for civil office, or too scandalous for the ministry of the English Church.*

Blunders of the English Government.

But this was a system for which William III. was not responsible. The evil and the obloquy must remain with the English Parliament and the English Governments of last century.

That the policy of William III., in maintaining the Church of Ireland, was one eminently fitted to reclaim and civilize that wild population, is a proposition which we maintain before the world, and its evidence appears clearly in the incidents of the last half century and the facts before our eyes. Mr. Gladstone has spoken of the Irish Church as a failure. His statement is inconsistent with the facts; however strong his prejudices, the facts of history rebuke him. He will hardly say that the Irish Church is responsible for the vices of the English Government. Was it responsible for the blunders of Elizabeth's ministers in requiring that the Church services should be read in English, and the Bible be circulated in English, a tongue which the Irish could not understand? Was it responsible for the plunder of tithes, the abstraction of tithe agistment, the ruin of churches, the demolition of glebe houses, the union of livings, and the scandalous choice of Bishops? These however were the obstacles which thwarted the operations of the Irish Church from the Reformation down to the last half century. Can any rational man imagine that, under such a system, worked by such a Government, any Church could thrive?

Revival in England and Ireland.

But at last there came a revival; not to Ireland only, but to England; not to the Church of England alone, but to all sects and Churches; the great revival of the last century, and that revival, as it awoke the Wesleyans and the Established Churches of England and Scotland, so it reached and touched the Church of Ireland. To its effects on the Irish clergy Mr. Gladstone himself bears reluctant witness. He has been forced to render testimony to the piety and zeal of the Irish clergy. These qualities in a body of clergy are gradual in their advent. They spread slowly. A Church does not pass in a moment from darkness to dawn. But what a body of such clergy might have effected, had they been at work in Ireland ever since the Revolution with the same energy and patience which has marked them in the last thirty years, is a matter of easy calculation. Scripture-readers, Irish Bible-readers, Sunday-schools,

* See the biting sarcasms of Swift, and the remarks of Sir Arthur Wellesley, when Irish Secretary.

day-schools, lectures, sermons, publications, the circulation of the Bible; these are their works, and the results are before us. The more palpable may be given in a few sentences.

1st. The Irish national schools are now teaching 910,000 children: allow a large deduction for fraudulent returns and sham-teaching under bad teachers. Still above half a million of Roman Catholic children receive an effective secular education. Yet, Dr. Cullen tells us, the system of the National Schools (viz., mixed education under well-trained teachers in a secular training school) is an abomination* in the eyes of the Church of Rome. Yet, notwithstanding this dislike felt by the priests to the system, its benefits, valuable to the people, have been enjoyed for thirty-five years with the consent of the priests, because they saw that the desire for education, *implanted by the efforts of the Protestant clergy*, had become so strong that they could not repress and dared not resist it. In spite of this education there are yet in Ireland *more than a million and a half* who can't read or write. What a state of barbarism would Ireland have been in now, had the priests had their way and the Protestant Church not existed! The stimulus of the Protestant clergy, the competition of Protestant schools, the establishment of good secular schools, have rescued *two thirds of the Romish population* from brutal ignorance.† This is the first result of a Protestant Church.

2nd. Speaking to Englishmen I need not dwell on the benefits of the circulation of the Bible. Looking only to its social results, the circulation of such a standard of truth elevates the wildest nation. In every Romish country the Bible is unknown, except by the small educated class. Generally, it is confined to the priesthood. It is unknown in Rome, in Spain, and in Belgium, little known in France, except through the partial efforts of the Protestants. But it is now‡ widely circulated in Ireland—in a Protestant and a Roman Catholic version, and its circulation is due

National effects of the Irish Church.

---

* The last expression of this feeling is given by Dr. M'Hale at Castlebar, Co. Mayo ("Freeman's Journal," August 8, 1868). He is speaking of Protestant and liberal landlords: "These gentlemen insist on the schools being vested in themselves, or transferred to that anti-Catholic Association, the National, or rather anti-National, Board."

† I quite admit the serious defects of the National Board system. The English inspector saw that it does not restrain from crime. The proof is that in English gaols the great body of criminals are illiterate, in Irish gaols a far larger proportion can read and write. (See Dr. Handcock's "Judicial Statistics of Ireland.")

‡ See Archbishop Whately's testimony. (Senior's Journals, Vol. II. p. 64.)

solely to the efforts of the Protestant clergy, and the laity combined with them, who have so diffused a taste for it, and a popular curiosity, that its circulation became indispensable.

3d. The effects on the social condition of Ireland are no less visible. Mr. Bright proposes* to undo all that has been done—to turn the engine backwards. Nothing is easier. The ascent to partial civilization, like that on the Mont Cenis, has been slow and difficult. Reverse the engine, and the train will roll to the bottom in hopeless wreck.

An eminent Irish Barrister has given us a graphic picture of the condition of the Irish tenants or cottiers in his younger days at the close of the last century.† The rental paid by the tenant averaged 3*l*.—the acreage, averaged five to six acres; the laws‡ of George II. compelled landlords to multiply a swarm of wretched cottiers; the cabins were indescribable from filth, smoke, and sloth; the implements of agriculture were such as we saw in the Scotch Highlands fifty years ago; the cabins, such as Mr. Matheson found, thirty years ago, in the Isle of Lewis, and, as some of us remember, in the hovels of St. Kilda; starvation fell on the cattle§ periodically in winter, on their families periodically at Midsummer. This was the normal condition of three provinces of Ireland at the beginning of this century. Lord Mayo's facts, stated last Session, and uncontradicted, mark the progress. This progress has been (as Mr. Senior shows) due to the capital, the intelligence, and the *restrictions* of the landlords‖; Ireland would recede into its old condition of barbarism, were these restraints and these stimulants withdrawn. Mr. Bright proposes to cut them off with his reckless tomahawk; they would cease without this blow, were Ireland handed over to the dominion of the priests. For such a Government would make it hazardous and useless for intelligent landlords to remain.¶

* Vide Mr. Bright's speech at Limerick.

† Ireland. By Gerald Fitzgibbon, Esq., one of the Masters in Chancery in Ireland, 1868. Pp. 125, 6.

‡ Fitzgibbon, p. 129.

§ Fitzgibbon, p. 141.

‖ Senior. Journals. Vol. I., p. 295.

¶ An estate in Galway, says one of Mr. Senior's informants, "is now one of the best-conditioned estates in Ireland. I found it in a frightful state, all in rundale, cut into patches distributed among the tenants, who, without the landlord's consent, or even knowledge, sold, mortgaged, and exchanged among one another, and so scattered that a farm of ten acres had to be looked for at ten different places. . . . Of course I met with much opposition. Every man thought himself injured. . . . Now, they admit they are better off."

Then the Emerald Isle would become like the Roman Campagna, a land favoured in soil and sky, but blighted into sterility by the Papal Government. Would any landlord remain on his property when* Cardinal Cullen and the Bishops were the rulers? Could any landlord venture to improve his property, or raise the condition of the peasants,† when the priest was near to denounce him? Would any manufacturer introduce capital, or invest his fortune in a country where priestly denunciations, priestly exactions, and priestly holidays prevailed, where a hint from the altar brought the Ribbonmen to burn down the farm or cottage, or shot down the offender at mid-day, when not a soul would give evidence of the crime?

Would that be ‡ a country for capitalists, or landlords, or improving tenants? A hunger-bitten, slothful, hopeless swarm would cover the half-tilled soil, and as the population grew, so would grow the fees of the priests, and the misery of the people.

4th. I put last, as of least importance, the actual number of Protestants now in Ireland. These amount to 693,357, members of the Church; Presbyterians and other Protestants, 645,351 — or

Government of Priests in Ireland.

"How did the Priests act? Opposed me to the utmost, *as they do every improver* and every improvement. They have no sympathy for comfort, or cleanliness, or prudence. All that they desire is *population*, christenings, marriages, *dues, and fees.*" Senior. Vol. II., p. 83.

* "True, Archbishop Cullen, who is Ultramontane, is converting their Church into a monarchy, with the Pope for its King, himself for its Viceroy." —Senior. Vol. II., pp. 114—183.

† "If I were to buy an estate of 500*l.* or 600*l.* a-year in Ireland, I could not reside on it. I should find no security; I should be hated by my tenants, calumniated by the priest, and perhaps should expose my wife and children to danger if I ever went out with them. Such at least would be my fate, unless I consented to let the tenants have their own way, mismanage and divide the land, and multiply into a swarm of wretched proletaires."—Senior. Vol. I., p. 297. Vol. II., pp. 116—117.

‡ " We are under two different and repugnant systems of law. One is enacted by Parliament, and enforced by the courts; the other is concocted in the whiskyshop, and executed by the assassin; and the law of the people is far better enforced than that of the Government. . . . The popular law, therefore, is obeyed; the Government law is disregarded. Give us merely security, &c."— P. 39. In the north " we have a worse element and a worse soil than in the south, but we have security. Crime is vigorously repressed, and the country is prosperous."—See Senior's Journals. Vol. II., pp. 34, 39, 41.

Reduction of number of Protestants.

1,300,000 Protestants. Now, observe the disadvantages with which Protestantism has had to contend. First, the massacre of 1641 cut off *one-third* of the then Protestant population. Secondly, the census of 1731 shows the Protestants to have been a little above half a million; and a fever of emigration, confined to them, carried off *one-third* of the Protestants between 1728 and 1768. Thirdly, the emigration before 1846 was confined almost entirely to Protestants, from causes which are easily explained (see Hobart Seymour's "Letter to Earl of Derby," p. 20-1), and the emigration is supposed to have carried off 150,000 Protestants, before the general exodus began. In that exodus, the emigrants from Ulster were rather above their proportion.

The emigration (it has been argued) fell chiefly on Roman Catholics. This misstatement is exposed by Dr. Handcock in his report to the Lord-Lieutenant. He says the emigration affected all alike—Celtic, English, and Scotch settlers equally. Statistics prove this; for from May, 1851, to December, 1867, the emigrants from Ireland were 1,832,000, and of these 480,000 came from Ulster.

But, besides this, the emigration had affected *Protestant converts* with peculiar force. Take as an illustration one district—West Connaught—the census shows that in a population of 131,529, the increase of Protestants between 1834 and 1861 was 3,640, yet it would have been 6,000 but for the emigration. To test this, the Rev. W. Plunket traced the cases of 164 converts, and found that 88 had left the district, and that persecution caused them to fly.

Yet in spite of all these causes, lowering the Protestant population, the Parliamentary census answers Mr. Gladstone. It shows a slow but steady progress of the Protestant population in Ireland. In 1834 every 100 of the Irish population were thus classed—81 Roman Catholics to 19 Protestants; 1861, 78 Roman Catholics to 22 Protestants. Nor is it less notable that on the register of national schools in 1867, there were 175,000 Protestants, and in Church Education schools 56,000 more. Let any Government secure the freedom of the Irish people from the tyranny of the priests, the next census will show the proportion of Protestants to Papists still further changed.

5th. But this gives an inadequate view of the benefits of a Protestant Church. It rallies and it retains above a million of Protestants. It is the breakwater that protects the coast against the destructive sand; it is the terrace-wall on the hill-side, that retains the earth, which would otherwise slip. This is its power. Take this barrier away, and I agree with Mr. Bright, you will undo all that has been done for 50 years; the want, and sloth, and filth, and famine, and fever, which raged in the course of last century, will return. Hopeless indolence, Celtic idleness, Celtic unthrift, cottiers' holdings, smoky cabins, dirty habits, swarming families, growing divisions of land, a hunger-bitten, priest-ridden, starving, yet highly taxed population; add to these faction fights, and Ribbon lodges, and raids of Blackfeet and Whitefeet, a reign of terror, and a dance of death; a country without law, save the law of the Ribbonmen, and without a Government, except the caprice, lust, and avarice of the Priesthood.

This will be the state of Ireland, when Mr. Bright's scheme has prevailed. Terrible as is the desolation of the Romagna, cruel as is the tyranny in Rome, pestilent as is the raid of Italian brigands, hateful as is the rule of Roman mercenaries, Ireland will be worse than the Romagna—more sterile, because less favoured by climate, more hunger-stricken, because from the eager division of the soil, the population will swarm in yet denser numbers.

This is the condition which Dr. Manning proposes to restore in Ireland.* This is the law, "anterior and superior to all human and civil law," which he seeks to replace. This is his reparation for centuries of wrong. He would sweep out the Protestant landlords,† give back to the Romish Church‡ the

---

* Dr. Manning's Letter to Earl Grey, p. 28.

† The *Tablet* betrays this part of the plan:—"We have always thought that it could be shown that, if the Irish Church Establishment were abolished to-morrow—if its churches, lands, and rent-charges were applied to secular purposes or even to Catholic purposes—or if, leaving the Protestant Establishment alone, the Catholic Church were endowed by the State, and put on a footing of perfect equality of wealth and privilege with the Protestant Church, we should only have dealt with one feature, with one symptom of the disease, and should not have reached the seat of the disorder. The wound of Ireland is, that whereas the great majority of the population of Ireland are Catholics, *such a large proportion of the soil of Ireland belongs to Protestants*, and that Protestants form such a large proportion of those classes which, by superior wealth and superior advantages, are raised in social station higher than the rest.

"This we believe to be the root of the Irish evil, and it lies deeper, far deeper, than the Irish Protestant Church Establishment."

‡ Dr. Manning's Letter to Earl Grey, p. 25.

property now held by them and the Protestant Establishment; and cover the rest of the land with a starving peasantry: this, he assures us, is the justice which England owes to Ireland.*

Do I exaggerate? The Romish bishops and priests have frankly told us what they intend. They told us this in 1843, when a rising seemed near. They told it in 1848, when Continental troubles threatened English disorders.

Read their words, and then say if those who predict peace from our present policy are not either culpably ignorant or wilfully blind.

Take the words from the columns of the *Times* :—

I.—Hear, first, the opinion which the Romish Church has of the English Government.

(1.) The Roman Catholic Archbishop of Cashel addressed the Lord Lieutenant (*Times*, Dec. 30, 1847), and accused the English Government of taking away by famine the lives of the Irish people!

(2.) The Roman Catholic Archbishop of Tuam (Dec. 17, 1847) charged Lord John Russell with trampling on the lives of six millions of Irishmen!

(3.) The Priest of Fermoy says :—

"I will not tamely surrender my rights; neither do I intend to abandon the political arena, while the religion and lives of the people are exposed to the insults and treachery of an *inimical Government*. The cause of the people is that of the priests; the priests will be ever at their posts when the lives of the people are in danger, either from famine, from pestilence, or the *sword of the Tyrant*."

He refers to the dethroning of Louis Philippe, and says that *resistance to oppression* is equally a virtue in Ireland as on the Continent (March 30, 1848).

(4.) The Rev. Dr. O'Brien (April 3, 1848) says :—

"God has sanctified the national will, by the miraculous triumph of the European Continent. Ireland's opportunity has been sought for forty-eight years. . . . What is your will? Is it to be governed by the incapacity of the Commons and the anility of the incurable Lords? You have, in every form, set forth your will that your native land had outgrown the state of pupillage and provincialism. If power constitutes the right of ruling, subjection is only the *necessity of weakness;* allegiance will have vanished *as soon as the vassal is able to strike down the king*."

(5.) The *Times* (April 15, 1848) :—

"At a meeting of the Saarsfield Club, Mr. O'Donnell recom-

* Dr. Manning's Letter to Earl Grey, p. 44.

mended depositors in banks to withdraw their capital. The Rev. Mr. O'Connor recommended *the people to arm.*

(6.) Father Kenyon, at Temple Derry Meeting, says :—

"You should counsel, advise, and direct Irishmen in general *to get arms* to defend themselves."

(7.) Rev. Mr. Birmingham (*Nation*, April 14, 1848) :—

"The English Government—which, after deliberately starving hundreds of thousands of you, I look upon as capable of anything—may tempt you to a precipitate committal of your cause to a doubtful issue ; but resist by patience the temptation. When the day of your struggle shall come, when your liberties as well as your lives shall be invaded, then let it not be a turning-out of two or three counties, but *let Ireland rise to the contest as one man*, and let every man make a vow to the following effect—'I vow before God and my country *to lessen, if I can, by one man at least, the enemies of my native land,* and to die."

The *Times* says (April 8, 1848) :—

"The excitement progresses ; the Roman Catholic Clergy have resumed their old position of political as well as spiritual pastors of the people ; they are to be found at every meeting. At Derry nearly every second speaker was a priest ; the same may be said of Limerick, Tipperary, and Galway, where the most inflammatory language was uttered by these reverend gentlemen in the presence of monster assemblages, ripe and ready to commit themselves to open insurrection against the Queen's authority." *The Romish Church for rebellion against England.*

Sir Charles Trevelyan (*Morning Chronicle*, Oct. 18, 1843) had written of 1843, what was no less applicable to 1848 :—

"There cannot be a doubt that the great body of the Roman Catholic priests have gone into the movement in the worst, that is in the rebellious sense ; some more heady and enthusiastic than the rest might even lead their flocks to battle."

II.—After such an exhibition, it is needless to say that the Repeal of the Union is held to be indispensable by all the Romish bishops and priests. We shall put this beyond all question :—

1st. In 1843, May 14, Dr. Higgins, Roman Catholic Bishop of Ardagh, says—

"I have every reason to believe—I may add, that I know—that every Catholic bishop in Ireland, without an exception, is an ardent Repealer."

2nd. Archbishop M'Hale, with 105 priests—

"Resolved that we commence the new year by enrolling ourselves members of the Repeal Association." (*Times,* Jan. 3, 1848.)

3rd. *Cork Examiner*—

"With feelings of profound satisfaction, we announce that the bishops and clergy of the extensive diocese of Cloyne and Ross have unanimously adopted an address to Her Majesty . . . . declaring that deep and general discontent exist amongst all classes, and a settled conviction of the utter inadequacy of English Legislation to remedy the evils of Ireland's social condition; they humbly but earnestly call on Her Majesty to summon her Irish Parliament in Dublin." (*Times*, April 15, 1848.)

This was signed by the Roman Catholic bishop and 140 priests of the county Cork, by the Roman Catholic bishop and priests of the county Waterford, and the Roman Catholic bishop and priests of the diocese of Meath.

The Romish Church for Repeal.

4th. A loyal declaration in favour of the Constitution was started in the spring of 1848.

"In Kerry," says Father Sulivan, "every Catholic priest, with the exception of two or three, *declined to sign it;* it was sent to the county Cork, and only one priest signed it."

5th. Whereas at Belfast the clergy of the Irish Church, of the Synod of Ulster, and of other Protestant sects, supported it, *but not one Roman Catholic priest.*

6th. Is this feeling changed? Take the last example (*Freeman's Journal*, Aug. 8, 1868). Castlebar, county Mayo. Archbishop M'Hale with his priests met to choose a candidate. They resolved—

"To give our strenuous support to those candidates only who can advocate the fullest measure of tenant right, unqualified freedom of Catholic denominational education, the disestablishment and disendowment of the Protestant Church, and, *above all, the repeal of the Legislative Union.*"

The two candidates put forward, Mr. Moore and Mr. Blake, were both ardent Repealers.

If after this England does not understand what is intended by the Roman Catholic hierarchy, she has herself to thank for her delusion.

What the Roman Catholic bishops mean by justice to Ireland is abundantly plain.

Fallacy of Mr. Gladstone.

On that expression, so much abused, I offer one word in conclusion. Mr. Gladstone imagines, that when you have proved that the Roman Catholics number four millions, and receive no help to their Church, while the Protestants only exceed one million, and yet keep a landed endowment, that the conclusion is clear. There never was so gross a fallacy, so easily exposed. If it is the duty of an imperial nation like England, to which are attached nations of a lower state and more imperfect civilization, to give all that the people ask, and to supply what they crave, then why have we put down human sacrifices, and the burning of widows, and the rules of caste in our Indian empire? Why do we pay Anglican Churches and clergy there for a handful of wealthy men? Why do we refuse to pay the Brahmins, and the Fakeers, and the Buddhists, and the temples of Juggernaut? Why do we hold India, when a vote of nine-tenths of the population, if taken to-morrow, would vote us into exile? Why, but because we wish to raise an inferior and a fallen race; because we regard our responsibility as not to be cast off, because an older State, with truth and higher intelligence, should no more desert its dependency than a father his child.

And do you mean to tell us, that when the Irish priests seek to divide Ireland into strips, cover it with swarms of starving peasants, tax them, rule them, and degrade them; when these priests hate us and our ways and our restraints and our capitalists and our landlords, and raise around us cries of hatred, and shout in our ears the shout of Repeal, do you mean to say, that to cast off a susceptible but improving people, to hurl them into the depths of bondage and suffering, that this is the duty of England, and the fulfilment of its mission? *Justice to Ireland.*

This may suit those preachers of justice and righteousness, who now are trampling on every principle of policy and truth, but I trust it will not suit the thoughtful representatives of the British people.

If we feel that to impose law, where lawlessness prevails; to raise to industry, when a rude race loves indolence; to rouse to effort, when a people would lie down in sloth; to govern the unruly, and protect the suffering, and guard the endangered, is the high mission of England in Ireland; then let us remember that without capital there cannot be progress, nor without security capital, nor security without law, nor law without morals, nor morals without the Bible, nor the Bible be nationally effective without an organized Church. If this be so, OUR CONCERN FOR IRELAND'S FUTURE PROGRESS is the real ground on which we maintain a Protestant Church in Ireland.

CHAPTER X.

THE FUTURE OF IRELAND.

The prospects of Ireland for the future are not doubtful if Mr. Gladstone's scheme of policy prevails. They may be described with accuracy, because they spring from causes now in operation, which obey the direction of a political law, that must come into full operation as soon as the Protestant Church is cleared from the area of Ireland.

I. The first effect will be, the Establishment of the Church of Rome in supremacy over three provinces in Ireland. The grant of money, which Mr. Gladstone is likely to propose, will supply funds. The Bill of Sir Colman O'Loghlen (April 30, 1867), followed by other similar Bills, will supply lands. In every part of the land Romish glebe houses, Romish churches, and Romish schools will start to view in unusual splendour. The scattered Protestant clergy, after a short struggle, will retire. Their churchyards (by the Act now passed) will be invaded by Romish mobs, interrupting the Protestant service and insulting the Protestant congregation ; and, as we have seen in a recent instance, interference will take place even with the interment of Protestants. If the clergy attempt to be active, they will receive, as Dr. Collis did, an intelligible warning. If this is not attended to, the steps will be taken by the myrmidons of the priest which characterised the tithe warfare, which led to the assassination of some clergymen, and to assaults on many. If any Dissenter (like the Wesleyan Mr. Campbell) ventures to preach, he will be set upon (as Mr. Campbell was), and dealt with unsparingly. In this way every whisper of Protestant teaching will be suppressed. The few surviving schools of the Protestant Church will be stripped of their Romish scholars; for a peremptory order will issue that no Romanists shall attend any but the priest's school ; and, if any children go to the Protestant school, they will receive the treatment* which for some

* See also Senior, ii. 70.

time was inflicted on our Mission children in West Galway, and in Dublin in the Coombe.

As the Lord-Chancellor will be a Papist, and soon after (if he exists) the Lord-Lieutenant, Romish magistrates, or Protestants as complying as Romanists, will fill the Romish Bench, and obey the orders of the Cardinal. Romanists will be the stipendiary magistrates, and the police, occupied by Romanists, will become the instrument of the priest's decrees. If any one, clergyman or layman, missionary or schoolmaster, appeals to the police for protection, he will be treated as for months our teachers were treated in Dublin, till Lord Palmerston interfered. If he appeals to the Bench of Magistrates, he will receive the sentence which has fallen on some of our missionaries in the West, "Serve him right." There will be a perfect unity in the system, and if any one ventures to complain of it in Parliament, the Papal band will burst into cries of indignation, and Mr. Gladstone, in mellifluous tones, will rebuke the Protestant sufferer and defend the Papal persecutor.

Under these circumstances the spread of knowledge or inquiry will be impossible; and the Protestants scattered through the three provinces, finding themselves isolated and unprotected by law, will leave a country which has become, like the Papal States, one in which truth is crushed and priestly tyranny rules. The converts, if any should still linger, will depart, and the drain of emigration will rapidly remove the firmer parts of Irish society.

The landlords will take the first opportunity of escaping from hopeless embarrassments, and will seek in exile shelter from dangers both menacing and intolerable. They will make the best terms they can, sell their lands, and convey their capital to other countries, where the laws give protection. As each withdraws, the secession of the others will become more rapid, till the stream has drained from Ireland the capital and intelligence which now stimulate improvement; and, when the supervision and the wealth which now repress barbarism are gone, the undoing of the past, which Mr. Bright proclaims, and which Dr. Manning with far greater foresight desires, will be accomplished. The restraints of landlordism, to which Mr. Senior attributes social progress, but which the priests denounce, will cease,* and the reverse process to that, which has been in operation for the

* Senior, ii. 216.

last twenty years, will set in. In place of larger farms, larger capital, and superior skill, the land will be subdivided into cottiers' holdings, and the strips of rundale, which we suffered from in the Highlands of Scotland in the last century, will each year become more divided and less productive, till the land, scourged by over-cropping into barrenness, will refuse to sustain in comfort a swarming peasantry. But these swarms will be stimulated by the priests, who now preach early marriages, and denounce emigration, because a swarming population secures their two objects—ample dues, and political power.*

If in the midst of these starving and swarming peasants any landlord retains his land, and ventures to reside, he will quickly, if he crosses the priest's path (as he must if he does his duty), find the fate of Major Mahon†; or, if he flies and leaves a steward behind, the pistol will reach him, as it has reached so many, the law will be powerless to discover the murderer‡, and the parish priest will pronounce over the dead a funeral elegy of invective, such as Lord Rosse has recorded of Father L———.§

Meanwhile, as landlords fly, and wealth departs, and capital is banished, and manufactures are closed, poverty will increase and misery spread, and pestilence on the heels of famine. Then the Romish bishops and priests will speak, as they spoke in 1847—8; archbishops will declare "that the English Government has taken away by famine the lives of the Irish people;" they will repeat the words of Dr. M'Hale, and tell the Premier, "that he is trampling on the lives of six millions of Irishmen." What Bishop Butler and his Limerick priests have announced, what Cardinal Cullen has hinted in his Pastorals, and Dr. Manning in his public letter, and all the Romish bishops in 1843, and the priests in 1848, will be poured forth in a concurring cry from every part of Ireland, that the English Parliament is incapable to understand, and the English Government unable to govern Ireland, that England must withdraw and leave Ireland to herself. Mr. Bright has told us that, when such a claim is made, he will advocate it, and Mr. Gladstone, facile statesman, will concur with Mr. Bright. But, if England should hesitate, Ireland will find armies ready at her call. Roman Catholic squadrons will hasten from the Continent in a crusade for the Faith; and from across the

* Senior's Journal, ii. 83. † Ibid, v. ii. 22, 41, 106, 116.
‡ Ibid, ii. 229.   § Ibid, ii. 21.

Atlantic will come the thousands who, Mr. Gladstone tells us, "are filled with a fierce resentment and inextinguishable aversion" to England.

The only serious difficulty will be found in the black North, for there lives in Ulster a hardy tenantry and a resolute Protestant population, to whom courage and union supply a strength beyond their numbers. They will not yield their necks to the yoke of the Roman Cardinal, nor present their breasts undefended to the pistols of Ribbonmen. But with this difficulty Dr. Cullen will deal. Before the final separation, he will represent to Messrs. Bright and Gladstone that the peace of Ireland is disturbed by Orange conspirators; and they will direct the Romish police, assisted by English arms, to coerce the banded Protestants and to protect the innocent Ribbonmen. They will ask Parliament for an Act to disarm the black North, and the Protestants of Ulster, disarmed and disowned, will leave a country which has ceased to be a home for them. Thus, when the English Government has trod out in Ireland the last sparks of patriotism, and when the North has been swept bare of its Saxon population, Ireland will pass, as a republic, with Dr. Cullen the Papal Viceroy, to hang on the flanks of England, to unite with foreign enemies and domestic conspirators, to use our weakness and prepare for our fall.

This is the future of Ireland, on the first steps of which we enter now. That future, flowing by necessity from our present acts, will at once vindicate the wisdom of our great statesman, William III., and will show in a clear light hereafter the infatuation of modern politics.

II. But what other policy can be pursued? What can you propose? The proposal is so simple that, were it not for party passion, it would be certainly adopted. For all that it needs is the capacity to read and learn from history, and the courage to act on the convictions of common sense. Two things are necessary for Ireland—first, to execute the law; second, to reform and use the Protestant Church.

I take the last point first, because it now occupies the public mind. I have no doubt, from the high character of the Commissioners, that their Report will be wise. But, writing entirely as an individual, and committing, and desiring to commit, no one else to the policy which I advocate, I should like to go further than they are likely to go, and to adopt a bolder, yet, I think, a safer change. I should treat the Protestant Church in Ireland as the Mission of England to a country inseparably united with us, but whose imperfect civilization hinders a full union. I should regard the income of the Irish Church* as a fund happily placed in our hands to enable us to spread Christianity and civilization amongst a rude people. Treating it thus, I should recall the Irish Church to its condition in early days, when Rome was a foreigner, and the novelties of Romanism had not been encrusted, like a leprosy, on the faith of Europe.

With this object, all rank and dignity and great episcopal incomes would disappear. No more lordly equipages, no palaces, no pomp of clerical display; as many Bishops as are needed for supervision, with limited and very moderate incomes.

But it has been said that there might arise an abuse of patronage —Bishops might swell their incomes by borrowing a leaf from the corrupt practice of the Church of Rome. Such a case should be rendered impossible; for the object is not to assign comfortable livings to lazy clerics, but to employ earnest men in a hard work. A Commission, one-half clerical, one-half lay, might be appointed to nominate the missionaries who are to give themselves to a laborious calling.

But, in order to make their mission effective, clergymen must be found, and, if the labourer is to work, he must not be left to starve. Therefore in every place where the clergyman does his work, a sufficient income should be provided. There are now many cases in the West of Ireland, in which clergymen, working hard, receive from the Church less than the pay of a common gardener, and are only raised, by an English voluntary Society, to the pay of a Manchester artisan. If the clergymen desire to open schools for crowds of children eager to attend them, they have no means. This is a scandal, but also a blunder; it is unjust to the Irish peasant who seeks to rise, but it is suicidal in the English Government whose interest it is to raise him. These cases abound, and these, if dealt with effectually, would settle the question of the revenues of the Irish Church. There would be none to spare.

Has a clergyman more income than he needs? Withdraw the excess. Has he less? Supply the defect. Is he doing no work? Let him remove, and let a zealous missionary supply his place. Is he doing a great work, and needs help? Supply it. Does he want a schoolhouse and a teacher's salary? Give him funds. This, you say,

---

* How did the wise genius of Dr. Chalmers correctly appreciate this. What a contrast to the sectarianism of Dr. Candlish and his friends!

will need an able Commission. Of course! But our condition is indeed deplorable if there are not to be found in Great Britain men who, as Commissioners, can be both honest and judicious.

But the duty of this missionary clergyman must not be *sectarian;* it must be national. Of course he will have his church and his Service—his church, Protestant; his Service, the Anglican Liturgy. His Sunday duty will be done under the supervision of his Diocesan. But there are six days besides Sunday, and on these he must work. In these his work may be as useful as his Sunday duty, and more immediately felt. For the people of his parish are Romanists, and will not attend his church. He must go to them, to their lands and their homes. He may instruct them in industry and cleanliness, and comfort. Their souls are the priest's; let the Protestant minister to their bodies. They are indolent; he may rouse them. They are thriftless; he may teach them. They are diseased or sick; he may help them. If he may not be the physician of their minds, let him imitate his Master, and take care of their bodies. The charity, which begins on the body, will soon touch the heart.

If it is said, this is a theory—yes, but a theory reduced to practice, tested by countless experiments, by missions of all sects and sorts, in all climes and races—among the negroes of Sierra Leone, the blacks of the West Indies, the tribes of our Indian empire, the Esquimaux, and the vagrant Indians of the Pole. If any man says that the Irish are more rude and inaccessible than these, he slanders them; if he says that Romanism is more impregnable than Brahminism, we meet him with facts. The experiment has been made and has been successful. Read the records of the Irish Church Missions, the evidence of unimpeachable witnesses—Peers, and M.P.'s, and High Church Bishops —not over friendly—reporters and correspondents of the *Times.* If, indeed, you carry to a Romish people dogmatism, invective, and passion, you will fail, and you deserve to fail. But if the charity of the Gospel fills the heart and touches the lips, it will baffle the bitterest priestcraft, and find its way to the human affections through all the fences of Rome.

III. But there is one thing more needful, which the Government ought to supply. That brings me to the other necessity of Ireland— the Supremacy of law. The English Law must govern Ireland. I do not mean extraordinary laws, or suspension of the Common Law; every man must be made to feel that the Law of the Land is stronger than he. In a savage country the violence of the strongest is the rule; the test of civilization is, that we are all compelled, whatever be our disposition, to obey the law. Therefore no man should be suffered to alarm or injure his neighbour.* If a Romish priest or Bishop denounces a man from the altar, and hurts his person or his trade, punish the transgressor and vindicate the law. If the priest's emissaries assault an innocent person, because he sends his child to a Protestant school, or attends a Protestant Church, give the sufferer relief, and punish his assailants. That is the duty of the English Government, but it is a duty which they have never performed; they have constantly evaded it. By compacts with Romish Bishops, by concessions to truculent priests, by secret bargains with rebellious leaders—by these, not by the Law of England, Irish Secretaries have sought to govern Ireland. Look at the result, see to what a state of insubordination this policy has brought Ireland. The only safety for England, as it is its duty, is to maintain the rights of all, and to execute the Common Law without favour, but without fear.

When this experiment has been tried and failed, we shall believe that Ireland cannot be governed by English laws. But the present attempt of Mr. Gladstone to make a bargain with the Romish Church, and to sacrifice Protestant endowments to an illegal confiscation,† that policy can have but one issue—and Mr. Bright sees that the end is near—to separate Ireland from England, to secure the degradation of the British Crown, and the dismemberment of the Empire.

* I asked a Frenchman in Normandy, what would happen, if a person was denounced from the altar by a Roman Catholic priest? He answered, that he would take the priest at once before the Juge de Paix, and he would be punished sharply.

† The clear argument of Sir Roundell Palmer is not more conclusive on this point than it is honourable to him: "It was not fair to disendow the Irish Church. It was not a question of competing clauses, but of mere confiscation."
—*Times*, Aug. 24 (Sir R. Palmer's speech at Richmond).

CONTRIBUTIONS to the NATIONAL PROTESTANT UNION may be paid to the Hon. Treasurer, Sir WALTER FARQUHAR, Bart., at Messrs. Herries, Farquhar, and Co.'s, 16, St. James's-street; or to Sir R. W. CARDEN, Hon. Treasurer for the City, Metropolitan Bank, 75, Cornhill; or Messrs. DIMSDALE, FOWLER, and BARNARD, Bankers, 50, Cornhill.

The Great Protestant Demonstration at Hillsborough, Oct. 30, 1867, Authentic Report ...	1d.
The Reformation in Ireland and the Irish Language. Two Letters. By SPES	1d.
The Church in Ireland. By SPES ...	1d.
A Few Facts, showing the State of Public Feeling in Ireland on the proposed Disestablishment of the Church. By an ENGLISH CHURCHMAN	1d.
Why is the Church in Ireland to be Robbed? By SPES ...	½d.
To the Protestant Electors of England, by an Ex-M.P. Three Letters, each	¼d.
From the Protestants of Ireland to their Protestant Brethren of Great Britain ...	¼d.
The Disestablishment of the Church in Ireland ...	¼d.
The Established Church—Unfolding of Mr. Gladstone's Designs ...	½d.
The Church in Ireland and Her Assailants. By RICHARD NUGENT, Esq.	2d.
The Clergy of the Church in Ireland weighed in the Balance, and the true Cause of the Condition of Ireland explained. By G. A. HAMILTON, Esq., M.P. ...	2d.
The Irish Branch of the United Church of England and Ireland ...	½d.
Speech of J. C. COLQUHOUN, Esq., at a Meeting in Defence of the Church in Ireland, at St. James's Hall, April 17, 1868 ...	1d.
Fallacies and Fictions relating to the Irish Church Establishment Exposed. By A. E. GAYER, Esq., Q.C., LL.D. ...	2d.
St. Patrick's Successors: Who are they? A Review ...	2d.
Is the Church of Ireland an Alien Church? Historically Considered. By Rev. S. A. WALKER ...	2d.
Speeches delivered at the Great Meeting in St. James's Hall, May 6, 1868, in support of the United Church of England and Ireland. His GRACE THE ARCHBISHOP OF CANTERBURY in the Chair. Authorised Report, Revised by the Speakers. Longmans, Green, Reader, and Dyer, London ...	6d.
Some of the Arguments by which Mr. Gladstone's Resolutions are supported Considered. By Lord REDESDALE. (Reprinted by permission)	¼d.
Justice to Ireland. By the LORD BISHOP OF CARLISLE ...	1d.
A Speech Delivered in the House of Lords by the LORD CHANCELLOR, on the Second Reading of the Suspensory Bill, June 29, 1868 ...	2d.
A Speech Delivered in the House of Lords by LORD REDESDALE, on the Second Reading of the Suspensory Bill, June 26, 1868 ...	½d.
The Proposed Disestablishment of Protestantism in Ireland; its bearing upon the Religion and Liberties of the Empire. By JAMES BEGG, D.D., Edinburgh ...	3d.
A Word to Dissenters. By the BISHOP OF CARLISLE ...	1d.
The Irish Difficulty. By AN OBSERVER. ...	3d.
The Church of Ireland—her History and her Claims. By ARCHDEACON WORDSWORTH ...	1s.
Scotland's Debt to Ireland. By the Rev. W. NIVEN, B.D. ...	2d.
The Progress of the Church of Rome towards Ascendency in England. By J. C. COLQUHOUN, Esq. ...	1s.
What is Establishment? Letters on the Church in Ireland, with a Preface. By J. S. BREWER, M.A. ...	1s.
Ireland in 1868. By GERALD FITZGIBBON, Esq., Master in Chancery ...	1s.
Votes of Members of the House of Commons on Questions relating to Protestantism during the Seventh Parliament of Queen Victoria ...	1s.
The Coming Election. How should Dissenters Vote? ...	½d.
The Church in Ireland and the Attacks on our Protestant Constitution. By W. H. KISBEY, Esq. ...	2d.

A reduction made on taking a large number for distribution.

C. A. Macintosh, Printer, Great New-street, London.

www.ingramcontent.com/pod-product-compliance
Lightning Source LLC
Chambersburg PA
CBHW031122160426
43192CB00008B/1078